A Looking Glasse
For London and England

by
Thomas Lodge and Robert Greene

An Elizabethan Text
edited by
Tetsumaro Hayashi
Assistant Professor of English
Ball State University

The Scarecrow Press, Inc.
Metuchen, N. J.   1970

Dedicated to

Dr. W. Leslie Garnett,
Dr. John H. Martin,
Dr. John Penrod, and
Mr. Nakagawa Nakaichi

Preface

This book is a revision and abridgment of my Ph. D. dissertation prepared at Kent State University, wherein I attempted to establish an authentic Elizabethan text of A Looking Glasse for London and England, an Elizabethan Morality play by Thomas Lodge and Robert Greene. Such a text seemed necessary because the oldest extant quarto A (1594) not only has two defective leaves (B2 and B3) but also includes some demonstrable errors and misprints; secondly, because the few modern editions which exist modernize the spelling and punctuation of the original play; and thirdly, because no revised edition has been published since 1932, when W. W. Greg published a facsimile edition.

To establish an Elizabethan text, I have collated the original quarto A (1594) with three major quartos: B (1598), C (1602), and D (1617) as well as with four representative modern editions: Dyce (1831), Grosart (1881-1883), Collins (1905), and Greg (1932). The result of my study accords with Instructions to Editors of the Works of Robert Greene, edited by Johnstone Parr and I. A. Shapiro in 1959.

Collation reveals that each of B, C, and D was on principle set up from the edition immediately preceding it, although it is not always a paginary reprint, and that A, which is the only edition supposedly printed from the authors' manuscript and thus closest to it, has the best authority.

The date of composition of A Looking Glasse seems to have been some time between April, 1586 and November 1, 1586. In that year Greene did not publish any work, and Lodge, as N. Burton Paradise argues, came back from his voyage with Captain John Clarke and stayed in England at least for six months until November 1, when he, as Edward A. Tenney claims, left for the Canary Islands and the Azores. This six-month period in 1586 seems the likeliest time for their collaboration, and suggests a date for the play much earlier than that proposed heretofore by critics of Greene and Lodge.

v

A Looking Glasse, an Elizabethan Morality play, based on the Book of Jonah of the Old Testament, stresses the sin-repentance-forgiveness theme, which reflects the preoccupation of their critics with morality in the late sixteenth century. The sources the playwrights definitely used are the Bishops' Bible (1568) and Lodge's Alarum against Usurers (1584). The contemporary reputation and popularity of the play are attested by Philip Henslowe's Diary (1592-1603) and Robert Allot's Englands Parnassus (1600).

Dr. Johnstone Parr, both as Director of my Dissertation Committee and as General Editor of the Works of Robert Greene, patiently and enthusiastically directed my work in 1967-68. Dr. John L. Gribben, a member of the Committee, took pains to proofread and verify all biblical and classical allusions in my work. The reference librarians at the Huntington Library, the Kent State University Library, and the Folger Shakespeare Library extended their efficient service to me in this project.

Dr. Reloy Garcia, Dr. Sidney Jackson, and Dr. Howard Vincent most conscientiously proofread the manuscript for me while this was in the dissertation stage. Dr. Thomas H. Wetmore, former Chairman of the English Department, Ball State University, and Dr. Dick A. Renner, present Chairman, kindly allowed me to duplicate a number of research materials through the departmental Xerox copying service. Mrs. Nancy Chalfant, my former secretary, most efficiently typed the manuscript for me. While I was revising my dissertation into a book, Dr. Louis Marder, my former doctoral advisor, who is now at the University of Illinois at Chicago Circle, gave me valuable instructions on the revision and publication. My wife Akiko has always given me the most needed moral support. It is to these advisors, scholars, librarians, and friends that I am deeply indebted.

Tetsumaro Hayashi
Ball State University
Muncie, Indiana 47306

January 1, 1970

Table of Contents

I. Literary Introduction

A. Authorship

The authorship of A Looking Glasse for London and England can be assumed by the fact that it is referred to as Lodge and Greene's play on the title-page of the four early quartos: A(1594), B(1598), C(1602), and D(1617). Moreover, the Stationers' Register specifically records the play (on March 5, 1594 and on August 14, 1600) as by Lodge and Greene. 1

B. Date of Composition

It is nearly impossible to determine the exact date of A Looking Glasse for London and England with certainty, but the approximate date of composition may be conjectured by a combination of internal and external evidence.

Grosart observes the date of composition to be approximately 1588 or before the summer of 1589. 2 Collins claims it to be sometime between the spring of 1589 and mid-August of 1591, or more specifically about 1590. 3 Dickinson sets the date between 1587 and 1588. 4 Jordan conjectures it to be before Lodge's departure for the Canaries in 1588, 5 while Gayley sets it before 1587. 6 Paradise claims 1587-1588 to be the likely date of composition. 7 Greg believes it to be sometime between 1588 and 1590. 8 McNeir argues that the date should be either late in 1589 or early in 1590. 9

Since Henslowe's Diary records the earliest date of performance of A Looking Glasse to be March 8, 1592, 10 it was obviously written before that date. Inasmuch as Henslowe does not record the play as "new" ("ne"), apparently it was classified as an older play at that time. Exactly how much older, of course, must be determined.

To arrive at a more precise date for the play, reference must be made to some passages in two prose

9

works of Greene: namely, <u>Greenes Vision</u> (published in
1592 but written in 1590) and his <u>Mourning Garment</u> (1590).
In the <u>Vision</u> Greene laments that he has been accused of
writing a scurrilous pamphlet entitled <u>The Cobler of Canter-</u>
<u>bury</u>, a work not entered in the Stationers' Register but
whose title-page bears the date 1590. Moreover, according
to the <u>Cobler's</u> title-page, the work was "an invective
against Tarletons Newes out of Purgatory," which was
entered in the Stationers' Register on June 26, 1590.
Therefore, the <u>Cobler</u> as well as Greene's <u>Vision</u> must
have been written after June 26, 1590. Furthermore, near
the end of the <u>Vision</u> Greene remarks that his reading
public would eventually be able to read his forthcoming
book entitled <u>The Mourning Garment</u>:

> looke as speedily as the presse will serue for my
> mourning garment... (sig. H1^v)

It seems obvious from this passage in the <u>Vision</u> that
Greene had not published his <u>Mourning Garment</u>. The
<u>Mourning Garment</u>, however, was entered in the Stationers'
Register on November 2, 1590. Therefore the <u>Vision</u> was
written between June 26 and November 2 of 1590. A
reasonable guess for the date of composition of Greene's
<u>Vision</u> is therefore August or September of 1590.

Now, in Greene's <u>Vision</u> as well as in his <u>Mourning</u>
<u>Garment</u> occur respectively two passages having a bearing
upon <u>A Looking Glasse</u>. In the <u>Vision</u>:

> They which helde Greene for a patron of loue,
> and a second Ouid, shal now thinke him a Timon
> of such lineaments, and a Diogines that will barke
> at euery amourours pen. Onely this (father
> Gower) I must end my Nunquam sera est, and for
> that I craue pardon: but for all these follies, that
> I may with the Niniuites, shew in sackcloth my
> harty repentaunce: looke as speedily as the presse
> wil serue for my mourning garment, ... 11

In <u>The Mourning Garment</u>:

> Entring (Right Honourable) with a reaching in-sight
> into the strict regard of these rules, hauing my
> selfe ouerweaned with them of Niniuie in publishing
> sundry wanton Pamphlets, and setting forth Axiomes
> of amorous Philosophy, Tandem aliquando taught
> with a feeling of my palpable follies, and hearing

> with the eares of my heart Ionas crying, / Except
> thou repent, as I haue changed the inward affects
> of my minde, so I haue turned my wanton workes
> to effectuall labours, ... 12

In A Looking Glasse (V, ii), Rasni and Alvida and the
nobles and ladies in the court, moved by Ionas' warning,
appear in sackcloth lamenting their sins and pleading for
God's mercy with their fasting and prayer. These passages
in Greenes Vision and his Mourning Garment citing the
Ninivites in sackcloth and Ionas crying for the Ninivites
to repent may--but not necessarily--reflect the scenes in
A Looking Glasse. The problem is that we cannot tell
whether the play reflects the passages or the passages
reflect the play. If reflecting the play, as I think they
do, then the play must be dated prior to the Vision and
Mourning Garment--that is, the play must be dated prior
to August or September of 1590. 13

    In the passage cited above from the Vision Greene
says he must finish his Nunquam sera est. This refers
to Greene's prose romance or repentance pamphlet entitled Never Too Late, published in 1590 and followed by
a second part entitled Francescos Fortunes, published in
the same year. We know, however, that Never Too Late
had already been finished when Greene was writing the
Vision because in the Vision Greene's conversationalist
Gower alludes to it as the best work Greene had produced:

> ...no Greene, marke Iohn Gower wel, thou hast
> write no booke well, but thy Nunquam sera est,
> and that is indifferent Linsey Wolsey to be borne,
> and to be praised and no more: the rest haue
> sweete phrases, but sower follies:14

Later in the Vision when Greene says he must finish his
Nunquam sera est before he brings out his Mourning Gar-
ment, he is almost surely referring to the second part of
Never Too Late, that is, Francescos Fortunes. The se -
quence of composition of these works in 1590 is therefore:
Never Too Late, Greenes Vision, Francescos Fortunes, and
The Mourning Garment. 15

    Thus Never Too Late was written in early spring
of 1590, followed by Greenes Vision, Francescos Fortunes,
and The Mourning Garment--all written or published in that
year. In addition, Greenes Opharion (entered in S. R. ,

February 9, 1590, published in the same year) and his
The Royal Exchange (entered in S. R. on April 15, 1590,
published in the same year) add to the number of Greene's
works in 1590. This does not leave Greene any time to
have composed A Looking Glasse in that year, and con-
sequently narrows the date of the play to the year 1591 (before Lodge sailed from England in August of that year) or
1589 or earlier.

Thomas Lodge made two voyages during these periods
when he could have collaborated with Greene in writing A
Looking Glasse--that is, between 1585 and Greene's death
in 1592. The first voyage is referred to in the Preface to
his Rosalynde (1590). Lodge says:

> Hauing with Capt: Clarke made a voyage to the
> Ilands of Terceras and Canaries, to beguile the
> time with labour, I writ this booke; rough, as
> hatcht in the storme of the Ocean, and feathered
> in the surges of many perillous seas. [16]

That he sailed with Captain John Clarke to the Canary Islands seems certain, according to Lodge's Preface, but the
exact date of this voyage remains undetermined. N. Burton
Paradise contends that Lodge sailed as far as the Canaries
on Sir Walter Raleigh's 1585 voyage to Virginia, a voyage
commanded by Sir Richard Greenville, one "John Clarke"
listed as one of the gentlemen on board. Paradise maintains
that this John Clarke is Lodge's Captain Clarke, and that
Lodge left this voyage at the Canaries returned to England
by another ship, arriving by April 1586, at which time
Lodge is mentioned as a witness in a lawsuit. [17]

E. A. Tenney, on the other hand, contends that "the
only known voyage of Captain Clarke is that which set out
from England on November 1, 1586, in the Gold Noble, a
250-ton warship."[18]   From Lodge's account they appear
to have gone to the Canary Islands and the Azores--special
hunting grounds for English seamen. No date for their re-
turn is given. The probability, maintains Tenney, is that
they sailed home during the summer of 1587. It is certain
that they were in England the following year, for in July
1588 the Gold Noble helped battle the Spanish Armada. [19]

On his second voyage Lodge sailed with Sir Thomas
Cavendish, leaving England August 26, 1591. [20] Lodge says
in the Preface to his Margarite of America (1596):

> Some foure yeares since being at sea with M.
> Candish [Cavendish] (whose memorie if I repent
> not, I lament not) it was my chance in the
> librarie of the Iesuits in Sauetun to find this
> historie in the Spanish tong, which as I read
> delighted me, and delighting me, wonne me,
> and winning me, made me write it. [21]

This voyage, on which Cavendish died in 1592 and was
buried at sea, was a disastrous one. Lodge probably returned to England on the flagship Leicester early (probably
January) in 1593, [22] as in February 1593 he is recorded
ashore in England "quarreling with his brother William over
their mother's legacy. "[23] At this time Robert Greene had
been dead nearly six months.

Obviously Lodge could not have collaborated with
Greene while on these voyages. According to Paradise,
Lodge was out of England in 1585, returning in April 1586.
According to Tenney, he left England in November 1586,
and returned in 1587 or 1588. Then he left England in
August (or May) 1591 and returned only after Greene's
death. Moreover, as we have seen, the year 1590 can
also be eliminated because of Greene's exceptionally large
production of other writing during that year. Furthermore,
between 1585 and 1589 Greene entered or published the
following works: in 1585 Planetomachia (no entry), and A
Funeral Sermon (no entry); in 1586, none; in 1587 Morando,
Part II (entered August 8) and Euphues His Censure to Philautus
(entered September 18); in 1589 The Spanish Masquerado
(entered February 1); Ciceronis Amor (no entry), and Menaphon
(entered August 23). [24]

Since Greene did not enter or publish any book in
1586, this year--between April and November--seems the
likeliest time for his collaboration with Lodge in the composition of A Looking Glasse.

C.   Collaboration between Lodge and Greene

A friendly association and mutual admiration between
Lodge and Greene seems to have existed at least by 1589
when Lodge wrote in French a poem in the prefatory material to Greene's The Spanish Masquerado (1589). [25] The
poem suggests Lodge's admiration and affection for Greene:

Le doux Babil de ma lire d'iuoire
Serra ton front d'un laurier verdisant:
Dont a bon droit ie te voy iouissant,
(Mon doux ami) eternisant ta gloire.
Ton non (mon Greene) anime par mes vers
Abaisse l'oeil de gens seditieux,
Tu de morteles compagnon de Dieurx:
N'est ce point grand loyer dans l'uniuers?
     Ignoti nulla cupido. 26
Thomas Lodge.

Translation:

The sweet resonance of my ivory lyre
Will press your forehead with a verdant laurel,
Eternizing your glory, whereof I rightfully
See that you rejoice, my dear friend.
Your name, O Greene of mine,
Endowed with life by my verses,
Causes seditious ones to lower their eyes.
You, a mortal, companion of the gods.
Is not this, indeed, a great reward in the universe?
   I have no passion for a worthless person.   27

This is the earliest written evidence of their intimate relationship, although they might have been close friends before this date. Furthermore, before Greene died in September 1592, he published Lodge's Euphues Shadow (entered in S. R., February 17, 1592) on behalf of the author who had been abroad with Cavendish. In the dedication to Robert Ratcliffe, Viscount Fitzwaters, Greene explains the circumstances of the publication of the book:

> ... it fortuned that one M. Thomas Lodge, who nowe is gone to sea with Mayster Candish, had bestowed some serious labour, in penning of a book called Euphues Shadowe: and by his last letters gaue straight charge, that I should not onely haue the care for his sake of the impression thereof, but also in his absence to bestowe it on some man of Honor, whose worthye vertues might bee a patronage to his worke, ... 28

Moreover, Greene writes in a letter "To the Gentlemen Readers":

Gentlemen, after many of mine owne labours that

> you haue courteouslie accepted, I present you
> with Euphues shadowe, in the behalfe of my ab-
> sent friend M. Thomas Lodge, who at his de-
> parture to sea upon a long voyage, was willing,
> as a generall farewell to all courteous Gentle-
> men, to leaue this his worke to the view, ... 29

These two explanations about the publication of Lodge's
Euphues Shadow further testify to their intimate relationship, Lodge's confidence in Greene, and Greene's loyalty
to his absent friend.

Robert Greene seems to be responsible for the
general organization and plot of A Looking Glasse, partly
because his Friar Bacon and Friar Bungay testifies to his
gift as a dramatist capable of a complex plot structure,
and also because Lodge, who seems to have written The
Wovnds of Ciuill War shortly before his collaboration with
Greene, does not reveal his structural gift as Greene does.

Moreover, Greene must have written the comic
interludes in the play because, as Professor McNeir pointed out, the picture of villainy and roguery in the comic
scenes of A Looking Glasse may be regarded as a possible
link with the Conny-catching series that occupied most of
Greene's attention during the last months of his career. 30

Robert A. Law assigns Act I, Scene i (1-158), which
depicts the courtly life, to Greene possibly because Greene
exhibits an amazing knowledge of historical geography, as
exemplified in his Orlando Furioso.31 However, I am
inclined to assign this section to both Lodge and Greene,
not only because as a traveler Lodge was at least as
experienced as Greene, but also because Lodge seems to
have collaborated in writing this play shortly after he returned from his first voyage in 1586. Thus both probably
had extensive geographical knowledge.

Act I, Scene ii (159-289), which depicts the lower
class life of the clown and his ruffians, can safely be
assigned to Greene, who testifies to his worldly knowledge
and his experience with the life of London in his Conny-
catching series. The picture of Adam and his crew of
ruffians seems to reflect Greene's humor, too. 32 Oseas
seems to suggest Greene's attempt to create supernatural
effects on the stage.

Act I, Scene iii (290-424), which represents the
middle class life of the Usurer, Thrasibulus, a young
gentleman, and Alcon, a poor citizen, may be assigned to
Lodge because as Collins, Gayley, Paradise, Sisson, and
others have pointed out, there are identical references in
Lodge's Alarum against Usurers (1594) and A Looking
Glasse. [33]

> Gent. I pray you sir consider that my losse
> was great by the commoditie I tooke vp, you
> knowe sir I borrowed of you fortie pounds,
> whereof I had ten pounds in money, and
> thirty pounds in Lute strings, which when
> I came to see againe, I could get but
> fiue pounds for them, so had I sir but
> fifteene poundes for my fortie: In
> consideration of this ill bargaine, I
> pray you sir giue me a month longer.
>   (11. 308-315)

Compare this appeal made by Thrasibulus, a young gentleman, to the following lines in Lodge's Alarum against
Usurers:

> Other worke by liues, as if such a one liue thus
> long, you shall giue mee during his or her life
> 10. pounds a yeare, for 30. pounds, and be bound
> to the performaunce of that by statute.   Other
> some deale in this sorte, they will picke out a-
> mong the refuse commoditie some pretie quantitie
> of ware, which they will deliuer out with some
> money, this sum may be 40. pound, of which he
> will haue you receiue 10. pound readie money,
> and 30. pounds in commoditie, and all this for a
> yeare: your bonde must be recognisaunce, now
> what thinke you by all computation your commoditie
> will arise vnto, truely I my selfe knew him that
> receiued the like, and may boldly auouch this,
> that of that thirtie pounds commoditie, there
> coulde by no broker be more made then foure
> nobles: the commoditie was Lute stringes, and
> was not this thinke you more then abhominable
> vsurie? Naie common losses, & the reasonablest
> is, for 36. pound for three months, accounted
> a good penie worth, if there be made in readie
> money, 20. pounds, naye passing good if they
> make 25. poundes, I haue knowen of fortie, but

> sixteene pound, and tenne shillings. These be
> general payments, and receipts, incident to the
> most part of the young Gentlemen that I knewe
> deale that wayes: ... [34]

The usury scene may well be a dramatization of the prac-
tice of usury Lodge personally knew in London. Lodge's
previous experience in court as a litigant in bond-making
cases may also account for his expert knowledge. [35]
Furthermore, as Sisson argues, there seems to be a
parallel between Lodge's Saladyne in Rosalynde (1590)
and the Usurer in A Looking Glasse, as the former, like
the Usurer in A Looking Glass, defrauds Rosader of his
hereditary dues, squanders his younger brother's legacies
and lands, and spoils his manor houses. [36]

Act II, Scene i (425-599), where the wedding pre-
paration is made by Remilia and where God's punishment
falls upon her, may be assigned to Greene, because he
employs the Magi in raising the arbor to conceal Remilia
and in directing the lightning and thunder that cause Remilia's
instantaneous death.   Since Greene fully illustrated his
fondness for spectacular effects in his Friar Bacon and
Friar Bungay, I suspect that he might have taken charge
of all the supernatural elements in this play.

Act II, Scene ii (600-770), the trial scene, may be
assigned to Lodge for the same reason I discussed in
connection with Act I, Scene iii. [37] Moreover, Lodge's use
of an Old Latin proverb in his Rosalynde may also reveal
his hand in this scene. Non sapit, qui sibi non sapit,[38]
which is quoted by Lodge in his Rosalynde, is also found in
A Looking Glasse: "he is not wise that is not wise for himself" (1. 655).

Act II, Scene iii (771-950), in which the clown and
his drunken crew have their brawl and their coarse buffoon-
ing in the ale house, again reflects Greene's touch. Alvida's
poisoning of the King of Paphlagonia, her husband, to prove
her love for Rasni may also be Greene's favorite device,
which is further explored in his Friar Bacon.[39]

Act III, Scene i (951-1059), where the master of the
ship reveals the veteran sailor's art, may be assigned to
Lodge because of his recent navigation. There is a conver-
sation between the merchant of a ship and a sailor concern-
ing the art of navigation.

Mer. And though the Sailer is no booke-man held,
He knowes more Art then euer booke-men read.

Sailer. By heauens well said, in honour of our
trade, /Lets see the proudest scholler steer
his course/Or shift his tides as silly sailers
do, /Then wil we yield them praise, else neuer
none.   (11. 1025-1030)

The master's account of their experience in Act IV, Scene
i (1378-1394), seems to suggest that Lodge was well versed
in the art of navigation and that some passages like these
in A Looking Glasse are more than likely the result of
Lodge's experience at sea. [40]

Act III, Scene ii (1060-1292) may represent the
joint authorship of Lodge and Greene.   First, the injustice
and cruelty Radagon exhibits to his starving parents and
younger brother may be assigned to Lodge, because his
own legal suit against his brother William would have
intensified his feeling toward a family injustice. [41]   Secondly, the portrayal of Alcon's wife Samia, a strong and re-
sourceful female character, may be the creation of Greene,
a "Homer of women." Moreover, God's punishment, in-
flicted upon Radagon, again seems to suggest Greene's
fondness for supernatural elements.

Act III, Scene iii (1293-1367), the scene of adultery
committed by Adam and the smith's wife may also be
ascribed to Greene's hand.

Act IV, Scene i (1368-1459), where marine technology
and incidents are told by the master of the ship, may be
ascribed to Lodge again, for the same reason I mentioned
in connection with Act III, Scene i. [42]

Act IV, Scene ii (1460-1508), where Ionas suddenly
appears out of the whale's belly on the stage, may be assigned to Greene because of his fondness for supernatural
elements.   On the other hand, Act IV, Scene iii (1509-1666)
reveals the joint authorship of Lodge and Greene.   First,
Greene seems to be responsible both for the fire carried
by the Priest of the Sun and for the menacing hand with its
burning sword.   Lodge seems to have written a flirtation
scene between Alvida and the King of Cilicia, because Alvida's love song is strikingly similar to Rosalynde's madri-
gal and Coridon's song in Lodge's Rosalynde (1590), stress-

ing both the wantonness of love and the agony and ecstasy
of it.
      Alvida's love song:

> Beautie alasse where wast thou born?
> Thus to hold thy selfe in scorne:
> When as Beautie kist to wooe thee,
> Thou by Beautie does vndo mee,
>   Heigho, despise me not.
>
> I and thou in sooth are one,
> Fairer thou, I fairer none:
> Wanton thou, and wilt thou wanton
> Yeeld a cruell heart to plant on?
> Do me right, and do me reason,
> Crueltie is cursed treason.
>   Heigho I loue, heigho I loue,
>   Heigho, and yet he eies me not.
>   (11. 1537-1550)

      In comparison, Rosalynde's madrigal in Lodge's
Rosalynde is:

> Loue in my bosome like a Bee
>   doth sucke his sweete:
> Now with his wings he playes with me,
>   now with his feete.
> Within mine eies he makes his neast,
> His bed amidst my tender breast,
> My kisses are his daily feast;
> And yet he robs me of my rest.
>   Ah wanton, will ye?
>
> And if I sleepe, then pearcheth he
>   with pretie flight,
> And makes his pillow of my knee
>   the liuelong night.
> Strike I my lute he tunes the string,
> He musicke playes if so I sing,
> He lends me euerie louelie thing;
> Yet cruell he my heart doth sting.
>   Whist wanton still ye?[43]

While Coridon's song is:

> A blyth and bonny country Lasse,
>   heigh ho the bonny Lasse:

> Sate sighing on the tender grasse,
> and weeping said, will none come woo mee? [44]

Act IV, Scene iv (1667-1735) seems to be Greene's work. In Friar Bacon there is a scene where a devil deals with Miles, one of the comic characters. This scene is virtually revived in A Looking Glasse.

> Adam. ... the diuell and I will deale well inough,
> if he haue any honestie at all in him, Ile
> either win him with a smooth tale, or else
> with a toste and cup of Ale. (11. 1683-1686)

Compare these lines with those in Friar Bacon:

> Miles. ... heres one of my masters deuils!
> Ile goe speake to him.   What, maister
> Plutus, how chere you?
>
> By my troth, sir, in a place where I may
> profit myselfe.   I know hel is a hot place,
> and men are meruailous drie, and much drinke
> is spent there; I would be a tapster. [45]

The comparison between Adam's statements and those of Miles seems to prove that it is Greene who treats a similar scene in A Looking Glasse. [46]

Act IV, Scene v (1736-1846) may be assigned to Lodge again, for the scene deals with the theft committed by Thrasibulus and Alcon, who now bring the stolen articles to the Usurer for a meager fee.

Act V, Scene i (1847-2040), in which the drunken clown meets the King and his courtly nobles and ladies, may be Greene's hand again, while the authorship of Act V, Scene ii (2040-2151) is more difficult to determine. The opening lines, spoken by the Usurer, are for the first time in blank verse, unlike all other prose lines spoken by him. It may be possible that Greene took over the scene, because there is the use of an evil angel who tempts the Usurer to commit suicide by offering him a knife and a rope. However, Collins claims that the opening lines are versification of a passage in Lodge's Alarum against Usurers.

> In that day the horrour of your conscience shall
> condemne you, Sathan whom you haue serued shall

accuse you, the poore afflicted members of Christ
shall beare witnesse agaynst you, so that in this
horror and confusion, you shall desire the mountaines to fall vpon you, and the hils to couer you
from the fearful indignation of the Lord of hostes,
and the dredfull condemnation of the Lambe
Iesus. [47]

Act V, Scene iii (2152-2238), the dialogue between
Ionas and the angel, seems to be Greene's writing, as does
the comic episode in Act V, Scene iv (2239-2312). Act V,
Scene v (2313-2409) may also be assigned to Greene because
there is a phrase, "Against the stormes of Romish Antichrist" (1. 2407) which does not coincide with Lodge's
Catholic inclinations in 1589-1590. [48] From a religious
standpoint, Greene's career seems more to represent Ionas,
who first hesitates to obey the command of God, while
Lodge seems to represent Oseas, who willingly obeys God.
Grosart assigns Oseas to Lodge and Ionas to Greene simply
because of the sequence of their names on the title-page.
But this reference does not prove anything convincingly about
their authorship. My conjecture is that both dramatists are
equally capable of writing the verse of Oseas and Ionas. [49]

D. Type of Work and Literary Background

A Looking Glasse for London and England is a
Biblical Morality in the same didactic vein as Greene's
autobiographical pamphlets of "repentance" and his "conny-
catching" exposures of the London underworld. Its debt
to the older Moralities is fairly evident. The play frequently denounces sins and crimes through the prophets
Oseas and Ionas. The main plot is supported by illustrative
episodes on the multiple settings of court, tavern, pawn-
shop, and street. [50]

If the Moralities are, as W. Roy Mackenzie defines
them, a series of allegories presented in dramatic form,
and if they have as their constant purpose a desire to
edify, [51] A Looking Glasse may well be classified as an
Elizabethan Morality with comic interludes in the clown
episodes.

If virtue and vice are presented as striving for the
possession of Man, and if vice has to resort to subterfuge
in order to win his temporary companionship, [52] A Looking
Glasse definitely has these elements, although the characters

do not bear obviously allegorical names. Radagon, a para-
site and flatterer, for instance, justifies Rasni's action in
the light of the divine right of the king. Whatever he ad-
vises the king to do assumes the air of righteousness.
Thus Radagon represents flattery and Machiavellianism. [53]

As Alan S. Downer argues, the character of the
Vice, the devil's deputy, is a major contribution of the
Morality. The Vice is the ethical opposite of piety as the
Devil is the theological opposite of God; he is a kind of
child of the Devil, and a dramatic adaptation of the court
fool or jester. He soon becomes completely humanized in
the Morality as a man playing the part of a rogue or mis-
chiefmaker. [54] In this sense, Adam, the clown, is the Vice
personified in A Looking Glasse, who later refuses to repent his sins and to fast when all Ninevites become genuine-
ly repentant enough to fast and pray. By his own logic
Adam justifies the cause of his stealing his master's wife
and beating the Smith for complaining about Adam's adulterous behavior. Thus Adam seems to represent the Vice of
the Morality play with his immorality, lechery, and later,
gluttony.

Rasni, who is not a bad king himself, is surrounded
by flatterers and parasites. Thus he loses his sense of
balance and yields to the temptations set up by them. He
is always given an incentive to incest, adultery, and injustice by his subjects, but especially by Radagon, who
acts under the guise of loyalty and righteousness. Thus
Rasni, too, represents Machiavellianism based on vanity,
arrogance, and immorality.

The Usurer, by the same token, can unashamedly
justify his inhuman, fraudulent acts; so can the judge and
the lawyer who accept the Usurer's bribe. But in the
Moralities Man encounters the true Virtues and is eventually
reclaimed by them. [55] In A Looking Glasse it is through
God's will and providence, and, more directly, through
Oseas and later through Ionas that ultimate repentance and
forgiveness are brought about. From these elements we
may classify the play not as a comedy but as an Elizabethan Morality. The comic scenes are employed to drama-
tize, first, the spiritual corruption of the city as its setting,
and secondly, the need of repentance and forgiveness. For
instance, the setting of the play is the microcosm of a
general corruption, not only of the City of Nineveh, but of
London, England, and perhaps the world in general. There-

fore the geographical setting itself has an allegorical signifi-
cance that is appropriate in a Morality play.

Especially after 1577 the Elizabethan drama faced a
determined group of opponents who condemned the public
playhouses as sources of all manner of evils, and who tried
to prevent others from frequenting them. At no time before
1577, however, did the London authorities try to banish
plays from the city for reasons other than those of public
health. Their attitude was, then, one of supervision rather
than prohibition. 56 Stephen Gosson's The School of Abuse
(entered in S. R., July 22, 1579) is a product of the age
that witnessed a series of attacks against the London stage
initiated in 1577 by John Northbrooke's A Treatise Wherein
Dicing, Dauncing, Vaine Playes an Enterluds. ... are produced
by the authoritie of the worde of god and ancient writers.57

Gosson's attack caused Thomas Lodge to write his
A Reply to Stephen Gosson's School of Abuse in Defence of
Poetry Music and Stage Plays, which became the first for-
mal defense of poetry and drama printed in English;58 Lodge
was then to engage in a personal and literary quarrel with
Gosson for five years. This exchange ranged from the
publication of Gosson's School of Abuse (entered in S. R.,
July 22, 1579), Lodge's Defence of Poetry and Gosson's
The Euphemerides of Phialo (1579), and A Short Apologie
of the School of Abuse (entered in S. R., November 7, 1579),
to Gosson's Playes Confuted in Five Actions (entered in S. R.,
April 16, 1582), and to Lodge's Alarum against Usurers
(entered in S. R., April 16, 1582, published 1584), in which
Lodge requested peace and reconciliation and obtained it. 59

The main objects of Gosson's attack were the new
playhouses, the Theatre and the Curtain, where music,
spectacle, and speech tickle the ear, flatter the sight, or
whet desire. 60 And yet his criticisms were not directed
so much at the actors and playwrights as at the misdemean-
ors of the audiences... such as prostitution, prodigality, and
idleness. 61 Gosson argues:

> To celebrate the Sabboth, flock to Theaters, and
> there keepe a generall Market of Bawdrie: Not
> that any filthynesse in deede, is committed within
> the compasse of that grounde, as was doone in
> Rome, but that euery wanton and his Paramour,
> euery man and his Mistresse, euery John and his
> Joan, euery knaue and his queane, are there first

acquainted and cheapen the Merchandise in that
place.... [62]

He further argues that since plays and music appeal
to the affection, the brute part of man, acting and music
reduce man to the level of the beast; thus the classical
stories were lies, and the poets who wrote them liars, and
those who sponsored or willingly exposed themselves to plays
were in league with the devil. [63]   Thus Gosson observes
that if his countrymen "shut vppe our eares to Poets, Pypers
and Players, pull our feete back from resort to Theaters,
and turne away our eyes from beholding of vanitie, the
greatest storme of abuse will be ouerblown, and a fayre
path trodden to amendment of life";[64] the entertainment
offered in the theater by these idlers... "straunge consortes
of melodie to tickle the eare, costly apparrell to flatter
the sight, effeminate gesture to ravish the scene, and wanton
speeche to whette desire to inordinate lust,"[65] Gosson
argues, is a threat to virtue.   It was this motivation that
drove Gosson to his attack, and it was the moral depravity
of the theater, rather than the plays themselves, that in-
spired Gosson's invective and led him to recommend their
total suppression.   He firmly believed that

> As in euery perfect common wealth there ought
> to be good laws established, right maintained,
> wrong repressed, vertue rewarded, vice punished
> and all maner of abuses thoroughly purged: So
> ought there such schooles for the furtherance of
> the same to be aduanced, that young men may
> bee taught that in greene yeares, that becomes
> them to practise in gray haires. [66]

On the other hand, Lodge made a direct answer to
Gosson's attack in his A Reply to Stephen Gosson's School
of Abuse in Defence of Poetry Music and Stage Plays.
Since the work was refused a license, however, only a
few copies, without title-page or author's name, went into
the hands of the public. [67] Lodge argues in his Reply that
poetry deserves honor and respect for its antiquity, that
poetry answers to a continuing need of human nature, and
ought not to be cast aside simply because a sect of "serious
stoikes"[68] dislikes it, that poetry combines pleasure with
profit, and that its function is "in the way of pleasure to
draw men to wisdome";[69] the greatness of poetry resides
in its divine source, which is one means by which the Divine
Will communicates itself to the human race. [70] Poets, thus,

"were the first raysors of cities, prescribers of good
lawes, mayntayners of religion, disturbors of the wicked,
aduancers of the wel disposed, inuentors of lawes, and
lastly the very fat paths to knowledge and vnderstand-
ing, "[71] rather than purveyors of evil.

Lodge's answer to Gosson's strictures on the abuses
of poetry is based on the premise that every virtue has
its vice, as he contends:

> Shall on[e] mans follye destroye a vniuersal
> comodity?---I reason not the al poets are holy
> but I affirm that poetry is a heauenly gift...
> If you [Gosson] had wisely wayed the abuse of
> poetry, if you had reprehended the follish
> fantasies of our poets nomine non re which
> they bring forth on stage, myself would haue
> liked of you and allowed your labor. [72]

It seems certain that what Lodge attempted to do is to
make Gosson look at poetry as distinct from the abuses
of it which were found on the London stage, a distinction
which Gosson and other Puritans found it impossible to
make.

Thus Gosson's main criticism and that of the other
Puritan attackers is that poetry is immoral, and that poets
are responsible for immorality. They not only attacked
the playhouses as hotbeds of vice, but also denounced the
lewdness of poetry itself. They, like Plato, urged the
authorities to banish the poets and playhouses from the
commonwealth. [74]

Lodge, like other defenders of poetry and drama,
developed the traditional argument that the purpose of poetry
is to win the mind from wickedness to virtue, that poets win
men to virtue by pleasant instruction, and that the end of
poetry is to teach and delight. [75] Thus we find that the defenders are as "moral" as their Puritan attackers, a fact
which is reflected in the didactic and religious theme and
tone of the play, A Looking Glasse for London and England.
It is this literary climate that both Lodge and Greene, as
University Wits in the 1580's, found in London, and it is
this challenge that both of them seem to have accepted as
they wrote A Looking Glasse in the following decade. [75]

A Chart of Collaboration Between
Lodge and Greene

(A Looking Glasse for London and England)

Act	Scene	Lodge	Greene
I	i	X	X
	ii		X
	iii	X	
II	i		X
	ii	X	
	iii		X
III	i	X	
	ii	X	X
	iii		X
IV	i	X	
	ii		X
	iii	X	X
	iv		X
	v	X	
V	i		X
	ii	X	
	iii		X
	iv		X
	v		X

E. Sources

      The most important source of A Looking Glasse for
London and England is the Book of Jonah of the Old Testament. As Robert A. Law has pointed out, [76] both the wording and the glosses of the Bishops' Bible show the dramatists' use of that version rather than the Geneva Bible.. or
any other Bible.. for details of the Ionas story, which
constitutes a major part of the play. The reference to
Lycas is a case in point. At the beginning of the play
King Rasni asks, "Am I not he that rules Niniuie, /
Rounded with Lycas siluer flowing streams" (12-13). Later
Ionas remarks: "Behold sweete Licas streaming in his
boundes, / Bearing the walles of haughtie Niniuie" (1497-
1498). The marginal gloss opposite the first verses of
the Book of Ionas in the Bishops' Bible reads, "Ninivie is
the greatest citie of the Assyrians, situated by the riuer
Lycus as Strabo writeth. " No such note or mention of
Lycas is found on the corresponding page of the Geneva
Bible. [77]

      Furthermore, the spelling of the proper names
supports the contention that the dramatists used the Bishops'
Bible rather than the Geneva Bible:

A Looking Glasse(1594)	Bishops' Bible(1568)	Geneva Bible(1560)
Ionas	Ionas	Ionah
Ninivie	Ninive	Niniveh
Ioppa	Ioppa	Iapho
Tharsus	Tharsis	Tharshish
Hebru	Hebru	Ebrew[78]

      And finally, the wording and diction in many pass-
ages of A Looking Glasse are closer to those of the Bishops'
Bible than to corresponding ones of the Geneva Bible, as
the following examples indicate:

    A Looking Glasse:
      "Thou hadst cast me downe into the deepe" (1480).
    Bishops'Bible:
      "Thou hadst cast me downe into the deepe. "
    Geneva Bible:
      "Thou hadst cast me downe into the bottom"

    A Looking Glasse:
      "On which thou neuer labour didst bestow" (2205).

Bishops' Bible:
  "About the which thou bestowes no labour. "
Geneva Bible:
  "For the which thou hadst not laboured. "

A Looking Glasse:
  "Full of compassion and of sufferance" (2183).
Bishops' Bible:
  "Merciful, long suffering. "
Geneva Bible:
  "Merciful, slow to anger. "[79]

The Book of Jonah is a prophetic work of literature
with three central elements: a main character who is a
prophet, a chiefly didactic nature, and a theme which deals
with the preaching of universal salvation.   The plot of this
prophetic literature is as follows: Jonah, the prophet, re-
ceives from God the command to go to Ninive, the capital
of the Assyrian empire, and there to preach to its in-
habitants that, if they do not repent and do penance, they
will be punished by God for their sins.   In order to escape
from this mission, Jonah boards a ship bound for Tharsis.
Hit by a violent storm at sea, the mariners suspect that
on board there is a guilty man against whom God's wrath
is evoked.   When they cast lots to determine who this is,
Jonah is singled out.   After he is thrown into the sea, in
accord with his own suggestion, the storm immediately
subsides (I, 1-10).   But instead of drowning, Jonah is
swallowed by "a large fish. " In the stomach of this monster he sings a canticle of thanksgiving, and after three
days he is cast up unharmed on the shore (II, 1-11).
Summoned again by God, Jonah then goes to Ninive, preach-
es in its streets, and threatens it with ruin if its citizens
do not repent.   Since the King and the people listen to his
preaching and repent, God does not destroy the city (III, 1-
10).   At this Jonah is so angry that he wants to die.   But
God teaches him a lesson, by letting a plant (gourd) grow
up quickly to give the prophet shade and then, just as
quickly, makes it wilt; if Jonah should be angry at this,
God has a right to be concerned about destroying a great
city in which there are more than 120, 000 innocent little
children and many harmless animals (IV, 1-11). [80]

There is hardly a single verse in the entire four
chapters of the Book of Jonah that has not been worked into the play.   Most of these verses are in the same success-
ion as in the original. [81] However, Lodge and Greene

elaborated and expanded the story and inserted several
comic interludes for dramatic effect.

   We cannot know whether Lodge and Greene derived
any material from literature of their time, as Paradise
suggests. Paradise reports that, according to J. P.
Collier, "a ballad called 'a looking glasse' entered to Richard Jones
on July 22, 1568, and that this ballad may have been a
source of portions of the play. "[82] He further notes that,
according to Richard Ernst Carl, there is another ballad
of about the same date and more illuminating as far as the
title is concerned as a possible source of A Looking
Glasse. [83] On September 5, 1586, Richard Jones paid
the usual sum of four pence for a license to print "a ballad
of nowe haue with ye to Ninive being a sonnet of Repentance
vnder the Wardens handes. "[84] Unfortunately neither of
these ballads is extant. [85]

   Paradise contends, further, that The History of the
Jews by Flavius Josephus, which Lodge was later to trans-
late as The Famous and Memorable Works of Iosephus,
a Man of Much Honour and Learning Among the Iewes
(1602), may be another source, because "the character
of Rasni, or Rasin, for example, appears in Josephus,
but not in the Old Testament. "[86] This seems a mere
conjecture, however, since there does not seem to be anything in the play that corresponds to Josephus' work. [87]

   Lodge's Alarum against Usurers, however, may be
cited as the particular source for Act I, Scene iii, Act II,
Scene ii, and Act IV, Scene v, because these usury scenes
seem to reflect the situation and trickery discussed in
Lodge's Alarum. Lodge, for instance, discusses one of
the usurer's tricks as follows:

> Other worke by liues, as if such a one liue thus
> long, you shall giue mee during his or her life
> 10. pounds a yeare, for 30. pounds, and be bound
> to the performaunce of that by statute. Other
> some deale in this sorte, they will picke out a-
> mong the refuse commoditie some pretie quantitie
> of ware, which they will deliuer out with some
> money, this sum may be 40. pound, of which he
> will haue you receiue 10. pound readie money,
> and 30. pounds in commoditie, and all this for
> a yeare: your bonde must be recognisaunce, now
> what thinke you by all computation your commoditie

> will arise vnto, truely I my selfe knew him that
> receiued the like, and may boldly auouch this,
> that of that thirtie pounds commoditie, there
> coulde by no broker be more made then foure
> nobles: the commoditie was Lute stringes, and
> was not this thinke you more then abhominable
> vsurie? Naie common losses, & the reasonablest
> is, for 36. pound for three months, accounted a
> good penie worth, if there be made in redie
> mony, 20. pounds, naye passing good if they
> make 25. poundes, I haue knowen of fortie, but
> sixteene pound, and tenne shillings. [88]

This is exactly the same trick the Usurer employs to ex-
ploit the poor in A Looking Glasse.

The major repentance theme of A Looking Glasse
is greatly dependent upon the Book of Jonah of the Old
Testament. But Lodge and Greene also frequently allude
to material in other books of the Bible. [89] Thus the play
is actually an attempt to produce a modern medieval
Morality Play directed at London.

Record of Performances[90]

Rd at the lockinglasse the 8 of marche 1591 [1592] ....
vij^s 91

Rd at the lockinglasse the 27 of marche 1591 [1592] ......
lv^s

Rd at the lockingglasse the 19 of aprell 1591 [1592] ......
xxiiij^s

Rd at the lockinglasse the 7 of June 1592 .... xxixs

A, 1594 (STC 16679)

Copies Located: Huntington (Kremble-Devonshire).

Title-page: [Ornament: two As and two swan-like birds
    facing each other around a vase that is surrounded
    with flowers] A / Looking Glaſse for / LONDON
    and / England. / Made by Thomas Lodge Gentleman,
    AND / Robert Greene. / In Artibus Magister. /
    [Device: Mck. 299] / LONDON / Printed by Thomas
    Creede, and are to be / ſold by William Barley,
    at his ſhop / in Gratious ſtreet. / 1594.

Colophon: None.

Collation: 4°, A-I⁴, 36 leaves unnumbered.

Ht: [Ornament: the same as the one on the title page]
    / A LOOKING GLASSE FOR / London and England.

Contents: Al: Blank (verso blank). A2: Title; verso,
    blank. A3: HT, text begins. I4v: FINIS. (B2, B2v,
    B3, B3v partially defective)

RT: (1) A3v-I4v, A looking Glasse for London /
    (2) A4-I4, and England.
    'Looking' instead of 'looking' A4v, Blv, C4v, D3v,
    E2v, F4v, G4v, H2v, and H4v)
    Defective printing in RT B2v and B3v
    'A looking Glasse for London' instead of 'and England.' C2

II. Bibliographical Introduction

A. Bibliographical Descriptions of Early Editions

Entries in the Stationers' Register

5 Marcij [1594]

Thomas Creede   Entred for his copie vnder
the wardens, handes / a booke
intituled the lookinge glasse
for London / by THOMAS LODG
(E) and ROBERT GREENE
gent............ Vj^d [Arber,
ed. , 645]

Thomas Pavyer   14 Augusti [1600]

[Block Entry]   Entred for his Copyes by
Direction of master white
warden vnder his hand wrytinge.
These Copyes followinge beinge
thinges formerlye printed and
sett over to the sayd Thomas
Pavyer.

viz

. . .

The lookinge glass for London
.... Vj ^{d}

. . .

[Arber, ed. , III, 169-170]

Signatures: Sigs. 3, b. l. Caps. with Arabic numerals

Type-faces: Text: black-letter with roman and sometimes italic for incidental use. The chorus speeches by Oseas and the stage directions are mostly in roman.

Notation: On the title-page John Philip Kemble has inscribed "Collated & Perfect. J. P. K. 1798, " and in the middle of the page "First Edition. "

B, 1598 (STC 16680)

Copies Located: Huntington, Bodleian (2), British Museum, and University of Chicago.

Title-page: A / LOOKING / Glaʃʃe, for London / and Englande. / Made by Thomas Lodge / Gentleman, and Robert Greene. / In Artibus Magister. [swash capitals A and M] / [Device Mck. 299] / LONDON / Printed by Thomas Creede, and are to be ʃolde / by William Barley, at his ʃhop in / Gratious ʃtreete. / 1598.

Colophon: None.

Collation: 4°, A-I⁴, 36 leaves unnumbered.

HT: [Ornament: the same as that of A, 1594] A Looking Glaʃʃe, For / London and England.

Contents: A1: Blank (verso blank). A2: Title; verso blank. A3: HT, text begins. 14v: FINIS.

RT: (1) A3v-14v, A Looking Glaʃʃe, for / (2) A4-14, London and England.

Signatures: Sigs. 3, b. l. Caps. with Arabic numerals.

Type-faces: Text: black-letter with roman and sometimes italic for incidental use; the chorus speeches by Oseas are in roman.

C, 1602 (STC 16681)

Copies Located: British Museum (Smith-Heber-Fitchett-

Marsh-Locker-Lampson).

Title-page: A / LOOKING / Glaſſe, for London / and
Englande. / Made by Thomas Lodge / Gentleman,
and Robert Greene. / In Artibus Magister. / [Device
Mck. 299] / LONDON / Printed by Thomas Creede,
for Thomas Pauier, and / are to be ſold at his
ſhop in Cornhill, neare the / Exchange, at the Signe
of the Cat and / Parots. 1602.

Colophon: None.

Collation: 4°, A-I⁴, 36 leaves unnumbered.

HT: [Ornament: the same as that of A, 1594] A Looking
Glaſſe, for / London and England.

Contents: A1. Title (verso blank). A2: HT, text begins.
13: FINIS.

RT: (1) A2v-13v, A Looking Glaſſe, for /
(2) A3-14, London and England.

Signatures: Sigs. 3, b. l. Caps. with Arabic numerals.

Type-faces: Black-letter, occasionally roman or italic.

D, 1617 (STC 16682)

Copies Located: Huntington, Bodeian, Boston Public Library,
British Museum (2), Folger, Harvard, Library of
Congress, Pepysian Library (Cambridge), Pforzheimer,
Victoria and Albert Library, and Yale.

Title-page: A / LOOKING / GLASSE FOR / London and
England. / MADE / By Thomas Lodge Gentleman,
and / Robert Greene. / In Artibus Magister. /
[Ornament: a reversed flower-like triangle] /
LONDON, / Imprinted by Barnard Alſop, and are to
be ſold at / his houſe within Garter place in
Barbican. / 1617.

Colophon: None.

Collation: 4°, A-1⁴, 36 leaves unnumbered.

HT: [Ornament: a crown surrounded with rose-like
        flowers and some leaves] A LOOKING GLA∫∫E /
        for London and England.

Contents: Alv: blank A2: Title; verso, blank. A3: HT,
        text begins. 14v: FINIS.

RT: (1) A3v-14v, A looking Gla∫∫e, for /
        (2) A4-14, London and England.
        C3, C4, E3, E4, G3, H3, H4, and 13, London, and
        England. B2v, B3v, C3v, C4v, E3v, and E4v, A
        Looking Gla∫∫e for

Signatures: Sigs. 3, rom. Caps. (G1 b. l. Caps.) with
        Arabic numerals.

Type-faces: Roman, occasionally italic.

Modern Editions

Alexander Dyce, ed. , The Dramatic Works of
Robert Greene (London, 1831), I, 55-140. [Copy-text:
A, collated with B, C, and D.]

Alexander Dyce, ed. , The Dramatic and Poetical
Works of Robert Greene and George Peele (London, 1861).
[Copy-text: A, collated with B, C, and D.]

Edmund W. Gosse, ed. , The Complete Works of
Thomas Lodge, Hunterian Club edition (Glasgow, 1878-1882),
IV, 3-70. [Copy-text: an unannotated reprint of B.]

Alexander B. Grosart, ed. , Life and Complete Works
of Robert Greene, The Huth Series (London, 1881-1886),
XIV, 1-113. [Copy-text: A, collated with B, C, and D as
well as with Q (n. d. , Chicago).]

J. Churton Collins, ed. , The Plays and Poems of
Robert Greene (Oxford, 1905), I, 137-214. [Copy-text: A,
collated with B, C, D, Q (n. d. , Chicago) and Dyce's

edition.]

Thomas H. Dickinson, ed. , The Complete Plays of
Robert Greene, Mermaid Series (London, 1909). [Copy-
text: A, collated with B, C, D, and Dyce's edition.]

John S. Farmer, ed. , A Looking Glasse for London
and England, Tudor Facsimile Texts (Amersham, 1914).
[The copy-text is B (1598) although it bears the date of
1594.]

W. W. Greg, ed. , A Looking-Glass for London and
England by Thomas Lodge and Robert Greene 1594, Malone
Society Reprints (London, 1932). [Copy-text: A, collated
with B, C, D, Q (n. d. , Chicago), and Dyce's edition.]

Present Edition: Based on A (Huntington); collated
with B (Huntington), C (British Museum), and D (Huntington) as well as with the modern editions of Dyce, Grosart,
Collins, and Greg.

B.   Treatment of the Text

The copy-text has been faithfully reproduced, but
manifest errors and misprints have been emended.   Any
editorial deviations from the copy-text, except those
specified below as being silently corrected, have been
recorded in the apparatus criticus at the foot of the rele-
vant page of the text.

The copy-text has been reproduced according to the
following principles.[92] (1) The original spelling has been
retained.   This applies to the old spelling i when modern
usage has j (as in ioy, iudge, obiect), and to the old spelling v for modern u and vice versa (as in vpon, loue).   (2)
The word-divisions of the copy-text have been reproduced
(as in no body, shalbe). (3) Elizabethan spelling variants
such as I for Aye, then for than, of for off, to for too
(or the reverse) have been retained.   (4) Spellings of proper
names have been reproduced exactly as they appear in the
copy-text, no matter how diversely.   (5) The end of each
page of the copy-text, excluding the catchword, has been
indicated by a stroke (/).   (6) The signature of each page

of the copy-text is given in the outer margin opposite the first words of that page. Signatures are given as A1, A2, A2v, etc., regardless of variations in the type-face of the original. Unsigned leaves have been given appropriate signatures without brackets.

The following alterations have been made silently: (1) Abbreviations such as yͤ, yᵗ, w ᶜ, wͪ, wᶜʰ, wᵗ, qd, a, e, i, o, u, have been expanded. (2) Long s (ſ) has been replaced by modern s, and vv and VV by w and W. (3) Ligatures (fl, st, ct, etc.) and the digraphs ae and oe have been reproduced as two separate letters, and accent marks over ee have been omitted. (4) Turned or damaged letters and punctuation marks, as well as wrong font letters and points have been corrected. (5) Obvious spacing errors which wrongly divide a word (hus band) or combine words (ofher) have been corrected. (6) Ornamental initials, italic and swash capitals, and factorums have been replaced by roman capitals. When these initial capitals or any others are followed by capitals, the letters have been replaced by lower-case letters. (7) Head-and-tail pieces and other printer's ornaments have not been reproduced. (8) The beginning of a paragraph has been indented when the printer of the copy-text has neglected to do so. (9) The text paper, originally printed in blackletter type, has been reproduced in roman type. Words originally differentiated by a variation of type-face have been reproduced in italic. (10) No attempt has been made to reproduce hyphens at the end of lines.

The punctuation of the copy-text has been reproduced except where it is clearly erroneous by its own standards or would mislead a reader familiar with Elizabethan printed texts. A comma at the end of a paragraph where a full stop is clearly correct has been emended. When a reader familiar with Elizabethan printed texts might have difficulty in following changes of speaker in dialogue, the initial letters of passages of direct speech have been capitalized, and commas before any initials so emended have been changed to full stops.

When a full stop precedes a lower-case letter or a comma precedes a capital letter, the necessary emendation has been made. Other capitals and colons, question marks, and the like have not been altered. No apostrophes have been inserted to indicate the possessive case or elision. All emendations of the punctuation have been recorded in

the <u>apparatus</u> <u>criticus</u>. Emendations proposed by another
editor and accepted by this editor have also been acknow-
ledged in the <u>apparatus</u> <u>criticus</u>93

Notes

(I. Literary Introduction and II. Bibliographical Introduction)

1. Edward Arber, ed., <u>A Transcript of the</u>
<u>Stationers' Registers</u> (London: Privately print-
ed, 1875-1894), II, 645; III, 169-170. See also
Appendix I. Key to Abbreviations: Quartos and
Modern Editions.

2. Alexander B. Grosart, ed., <u>The Life and Complete</u>
<u>Works in Prose and Verse of Robert Greene</u>
(London: Privately printed, 1881-83), I, 177.

3. J. Churton Collins, ed., <u>The Plays and Poems</u>
<u>of Robert Greene</u> (Oxford: Clarendon Press, 1905),
I, 138.

4. Thomas H. Dickinson, ed., <u>The Complete Plays</u>
<u>of Robert Greene</u> (London: T. Fisher Unwin,
[1909]), p. xlix.

5. John Clark Jordan, <u>Robert Greene</u> (New York:
Columbia University Press, 1915), p. 178.

6. Charles M. Gayley, <u>Representative English</u>
<u>Comedies from the Beginning to Shakespeare</u>
(New York: Macmillan, 1930), I, 405.

7. N. Burton Paradise, <u>Thomas Lodge: The History</u>
<u>of an Elizabethan</u> (New Haven: Yale University
Press, 1931), p. 143.

8. W. W. Greg, ed., <u>A Looking-Glass for London and</u>
<u>England by Thomas Lodge and Robert Greene 1594</u>
(London: Malone Society, 1932), p. viii.

9. Waldo F. McNeir, "The Date of A Looking Glass
for London," <u>Notes and Queries</u>, CC (July 1955),
283.

10. W. W. Greg, ed., <u>Henslowe's Diary</u> (London: A. H.
Bullen, 1904-1908), I, 13-15.

11. Grosart, ed., XII, 274.

12. Ibid., IX, 119-120.

13. McNeir, 282, suggests the date of the Vision to be early 1590.

14. Grosart, ed., XII, 235.

15. Mary Evelyn McMillan, "An Edition of Greenes Vision and A Maidens Dreame By Robert Greene" (Unpublished diss., University of Alabama, 1960), pp. xix-xv, 89-90.

16. Edmund W. Gosse, ed., The Complete Works of Thomas Lodge (New York: Russell and Russell, 1963), I. 4 (Reprint from the Hunterian edition).

17. Paradise, pp. 35-37. Paradise notes (p. 37), "Lodge appeared as a witness on behalf of his friend Leonard Shapton. His disposition was taken April 10, 1586." (P. R. O., Star Chamber, Elizabeth, 115/18.).

18. Edward Andrews Tenney, Thomas Lodge (Ithaca, N. Y.: Cornell University Press, 1935), p. 96.

19. Ibid., p. 97.

20. Paradise, p. 239; Tenney, p. 124. See also Pat M. Ryan, Jr., Thomas Lodge, Gentleman (Hamden, Conn.: Shoe String Press, 1958), p. 78, who gives the date of departure as May 26, 1591.

21. Gosse, ed., III, 4.

22. Tenney, p. 124. Tenney quotes J. D. Dasent's reference of Lodge and the other men's arrival in January 1593, which is based on the record that in February Thomas Lodge was ashore quarreling with his brother William over their mother's legacy, and that the Privy Council sent out the letter, dated March 18, 1593, to "the Maiour and officers of the Porte of Portemouth. Whereas Mr. Robert Dudley, esquire, hathe taken a letter of admynistration of the goodes of Thomas Cavandysh, esquire, latelie deceased at the seas.

There shalte notwithstandinge anie former letters
wrytten from hence about the gallyn Leicester, the
Roe Bucke, two shippes that did appertain to the
said Mr. Cavendish, to require you to cause the
said shippes with their ladinge to be delyvered to
Mr. Dudley or soche as he shall appoint to receave
the same. " [J. D. Dasent, Acts of the Privy Council, 1592-1593, p. 125--quoted in Tenney, p.
124n.]

See also Paradise, p. 41. Although Ryan mistaken-
ly claims that Paradise says it was on June 11, 1593
that Lodge landed at Bear Haven, in Ireland, a-
board the Desire, Paradise clearly states that it
is impossible to say in which of these ships--the
Desire, the Roebuck, or the Leicester Lodge
reached home, for his name does not appear in
any of the accounts, nor does he give any information [Paradise, pp. 41-42]. See Pat M. Ryan,
Jr. Thomas Lodge, Gentleman (Hamden, Conn. :
The Shoe String Press, 1958), p. 78.

Thus Ryan is wrong in his interpretation of
Paradise's statement about the arrival of Thomas
Lodge. Tenney's contention seems more up-to-
date than Paradise's, as he seems to have found
additional information about the arrival of the
Leicester and the Roebuck in Portsmouth.

23. Tenney, p. 124n. See also Paradise, pp. 44-45.

24. Cf. Johnstone Parr and I. A. Shapiro, Instructions
     to Editors of the Works of Robert Greene
     (Birmingham, England: The Shakespeare Institute,
     University of Birmingham, 1959), p. iii.

25. Grosart, ed. , V, 240. See also Collins, I, 138;
     Edmund W. Gosse, ed. , "Memoir of Thomas Lodge"
     in his The Complete Works of Thomas Lodge (New
     York: Russel & Russell, 1963 [Reprint of the
     Hunterian edition, 1883]), I, 22.

26. Grosart, ed. , V, 240.

27. For this translation I am indebted to Mrs. Ann
     Urban, my former colleague, at Kent State Univers-
     ity, and her uncle, a retired university professor

of French who prefers to be anonymous.

28. Gosse, ed. , II, 5.

29. Ibid. , II, 7.

30. McNeir, 282-283.

31. Law, "A Looking Glasse and the Scriptures, "
University of Texas Studies (1931), pp. 42-43.

32. Dickinson, ed. , p. li.

33. Gosse, ed. , I, 36-37. See also Collins, ed. , I,
140; Gayley, I, 405; and Charles J. Sisson, ed. ,
Thomas Lodge and Other Elizabethans (Cambridge: Harvard University Press, 1933), p. 152.

34. Gosse, ed. , I, 36-37.

35. Wesley D. Rae, Thomas Lodge (New York:
Twayne, 1967), p. 31.

36. Sisson, ed. , p. 157.

37. Collins, ed. , I, 141.

38. Gosse, ed. , I, 16. See also Collins, ed. , I, 295.

39. Dickinson, ed. , p. Li.

40. Gayley I, 405. See also Paradise, p. 144.

41. Sisson, ed. , p. 155. See also Edmund W. Gosse,
"Memoir of Thomas Lodge, " in The Complete
Works of Thomas Lodge, I, 5-9; Paradise, pp.
44-45.

42. Collins, ed. , I, 141; Gayley, p. 405.

43. Gosse, ed. , I, 29-30.

44. Ibid. , p. 136.

45. Collins, ed. , II, 74-75. See also Daniel Seltzer,
ed. , Robert Greene: Friar Bacon and Friar Bungay,
(Lincoln: University of Nebraska Press, 1963),

pp. 91-93.

46. Dickinson, ed., p. 1; Grosart, ed., I, xliii.

47. Collins, ed., I, 141. See also Gosse, ed., I, 51.

48. Paradise, p. 155.

49. Law, pp. 41-42; Grosart, I, xli; Gayley, I, 406.

50. Boris Ford, ed., The Age of Shakespeare (Baltimore: Penguin Books, 1962), pp. 57-58.

51. W. Roy Mackenzie, The English Moralities from the Point of View of Allegory (New York: Gordian Press, 1966), pp. vii-xi.

52. Ibid., pp. x-xi.

53. "Machiavellianism" = of, pertaining to, or characteristic of Machiavelli in preferring expediency to morality (OED); "Machiavellianism" has come to be a synonym for amoral cunning or for justification by power (Columbia Encyclopedia).

54. Alan S. Downer, The British Drama: A Handbook and Brief Chronicle (New York: Appleton-Century-Crofts, 1963), p. 36.

55. Mckenzie, p. ix.

56. William Ringler, "The First Phase of the Elizabethan Attack on the Stage, 1558-1579, " Huntington Library Quarterly IV (July 1942), 391. See also Edward Arber, ed., Stephen Gosson, The School of Abuse (London: Alex. Murray & Son, 1869), p. 57.

57. A Chronology of Critics and Defenders of the Elizabethan Stage:

    1577 John Northbrook, A Treatise Wherein Dicing, Dauncing, Vaine Playes or Enterludes. ...
    1578 George Whetstone, Preface to Promos and Cassandra
    1579 Stephen Gosson, The School of Abuse

1579 Thomas Lodge, Defence of Poetry
1580 Henry Denham, A Second and Third Blast
   of Retrait from Plaie Theatres
1582 Gosson, Playes Confuted in Five Actions
1583 Philip Stubbes, Anatomie of Abuses
1583 William Rankins, Mirror of Monsters
1583 Sir Philip Sidney, An Apologie for Poetrie
1586 William Webbe, Discourse of English
   Poetrie
1589 George Puttenham, The Arte of English
   Poesie
1591 Sir John Harington, A Preface, or Rather
   A Brief Apologie of Poetrie and of the
   Author

[O. B. Harrison, Jr., English Literary Criticism:
The Renaissance (New York: Appleton-Century-
Crofts, 1963), pp. vii-ix, 85-86.]

58. Ringler, p. 164.

59. Tenney, p. 72.

60. Stephen Gosson, The School of Abuse, ed.,
    Edward Arber (London: Alex. Murray, 1869),
    p. 32.

61. Ringler, p. 410.

62. Gosson, pp. 35-36.

63. Tenney, p. 74.

64. Gosson, p. 44.

65. Gosson, p. 22

66. Ibid.

67. Elbert N. S. Thompson, The Controversy Between
    the Puritans and the Stage (New York: Henry Holt,
    1903), pp. 73-74.

68. Gosse, ed., I, 3.

69. Ibid., I, 5.

70. Ibid., I, 13.

71. Ibid., I, 18-19.

72. Ibid., I, 19-20. See also Tenney, p. 78.

73. Tenney, p. 78.

74. Vernon Hall, Jr., Renaissance Literary Criticism: A Study of Its Social Content (Gloucester, Mass.: Peter Smith, 1959), p. 221. See also Plato, Republic, III, 398.

75. Ibid., pp. 220-221; and cf. Margaret Mary Cotham, "Greene and Lodge's A Looking Glasse for London and England," Unpublished M. A. thesis, University of Texas, August, 1928.

76. Law, p. 37.

77. Ibid., pp. 37-38.

78. Ibid., p. 38.

79. Ibid., pp. 35-36.

80. A. van den Born, Encyclopedic Dictionary of the Bible, trans. by Louis F. Hartman (New York: McGraw-Hill, 1963), 1198-1199.

81. See the Commentary which notes the Biblical analogy apropos of the proper lines.

82. N. Burton Paradise, Thomas Lodge: the History of an Elizabethan (New Haven: Yale University Press, 1931), p. 154. See also Collins, I, 185; Arber, I, 381.

83. Carl, Uber Thomas Lodges Leben und Werke (Hall: Druck von E. Kanas, 1887), p. 29.

84. Arber, ed., II, 457.

85. Paradise, p. 154.

86. Ibid., p. 154. As early as 1591, a translation of Josephus' Wars of the Jews had been considered.

87. Flavius Josephus, The Great Roman-Jewish War:
    A. D. 66-70, trans. by William Whiston, revised
    by William R. Farmer (New York: Harper, 1960).

    Josephus, Works, 3 vols., trans. by William
    Whiston (New York: A. L. Burt and Co., [n. d.]).

88. Gosse, ed., I, 36-37.

89. See the Commentary which refers to such Biblical
    allusions in the play.

90. W. W. Greg, ed., Henslowe's Diary (London:
    A. H. Bullen, 1904-1908), I, 13-15.

91. Amount of money recorded by Henslowe.

92. The direction on the treatment of the text is taken
    from the Instruction to Editors of the Works of
    Robert Greene which was prepared by Dr. John-
    stone Parr, Professor of English at Kent State
    University, and Professor I. A. Shapiro, Senior
    Lecturer at the University of Birmingham, England
    in 1959.

93. Parr and Shapiro, pp. 21-28.

III. AN ELIZABETHAN TEXT OF A LOOKING GLASSE FOR LONDON AND ENGLAND

A LOOKING GLASSE FOR

London and England

$\boxed{\text{I, 1}}^1$

Enters Rasni, King of Niniuie, with three Kings of Cilicia,   1 A3

    Creete, and Paphlagonia, from the ouerthrow of

    Ieroboam, King of Ierusalem.

$\boxed{\text{Rasni.}}$ So pace ye on tryumphant warriours,

Make Venus Lemmon armd in al his pomp,   5

Bash at the brightnesse of your hardy lookes,

For you the Viceroyes are the Caualires,

That wait on Rasnis royall mightinesse:

Boast pettie kings, and glory in your fates,

That stars haue made your fortunes clime so high,   10

To giue attend on Rasnis excellence.

Am I not he that rules great Niniuie,

---

[1]The act-scene divisions are those of Collins's edition. See the
Appendix II. All the abbreviations (A, B, C, D, etc.) are indentified
in Appendix I.

1: Rasni, / Rasni BDEFG(2); Rasin AC See the Commentary.
1: Cilicia / DEFG(5); Cicilia ABC See the Commentary.
4: / Rasni. / / CEF; omitted ABD; RASNI. Dyce
7: Viceroyes / CDEF; Viceroyes AB; viceroys Dyce
7: are / EG(Dyce)Dyce; and ABCDF
8: Rasnis / CE; Rasins AF; Rasnies BDG(2)
11: Rasnis / C; Rasins A; Rasnies BC(2); Rasinis DEF; Rasni's Dyce

Rounded with <u>Lycas</u> silver flowing streams,

Whose Citie large <u>Diametri</u> containes,

Euen three daies iouenies length from wall to wall,   15

Two hundreth gates carued out of burnisht brasse,

As glorious as the portoyle of the Sunne,

And for to decke heauens battlements with pride,

Six hundreth Towers that toplesse touch the cloudes:

This Citie is the footestoole of your King,   20

A hundreth Lords do honour at my feete,

My scepter straineth both the poralels,

And now to enlarge the highnesse of my power,

I haue made <u>Iudeas</u> Monarch flee the field,

And beat proud <u>Ieroboam</u> from his holds,   25

Winning from <u>Cades</u> to <u>Samaria</u>, /

Great <u>Iewries</u> God that foilde stout <u>Benhadab</u>,

Could not rebate the strength that <u>Rasni</u> brought,   A3v

For be he God in heauen, yet Viceroyes know,

<u>Rasni</u> is God on earth and none but he.   30

<u>Cilicia.</u>

If louely shape, feature by natures skill,

Passing in beautie faire <u>Endymions</u>,

That <u>Luna</u> wrapt within her snowy brests,

23: to enlarge / CFG(3,4); t'enlarge EDyce; to t'enlarge ABD
31: <u>Cilicia</u> / BCF; --. DEG(5); <u>Cicilia</u>. <u>A</u>; K. OF CIL. <u>Dyce</u>

Or that sweet boy that wrought bright Venus bane,

Transformde vnto a purple Hiacynth,   35

If beautis Nunpareile in excellence,

May make a King match with the Gods in gree,

Rasni is God on earth, and none but hee.

Creet.

If martial lookes wrapt in a cloud of wars

More fierce then Mars, lightneth from his eyes   40

Sparkling reuenge and drye disparagement:

If doughtie deeds more haughtie then any done,

Seald with the smile of fortune and of fate,

Matchlesse to manage Lance and Curtelex,

If such high actions grac'd with victories,   45

May make a King match with the Gods in gree,

Rasni is God on earth, and none but hee.

Paphlag.

If Pallas wealth --

Rasni.

Viceroyes inough, peace Paphlagon no more,

See wheres my sister faire Remilia,   50

Fairer then was the virgin Dania,

That waits on Venus with a golden show,

She that hath stolne the wealth of Rasnies lookes,

48: wealth -- / EDyce; --, -F; --. ABCDG(2-5)
53: Rasnies / CG(3,4); Rasnes ABD; Rasni's EDyce; Rasnis F

And tide his thoughts within her louely lockes,

She that is lou'd, and loue vnto your King,   55

See where she comes to gratulate my fame.

Enters Radagon with Remilia, sister to Rasni, Aluida wife to Paphlagon,

    and other Ladies, bringing a Globe seated in a ship.

Remilia.

Victorious Monarch, second vnto Ioue,   60

Mars vpon earth, and Neptune on the Seas, /

Whose frowne stroyes all the Ocean with a calme,   A4

Whose smile, drawes Flora to display her pride,

Whose eye holds wanton Venus at a gaze,

Rasni, the Regent of great Niniuie,   65

For thou hast foyld proud Ieroboams force,

And like the mustering breath of Aeolus,

That ouerturnes the pines of Libanon,

Hast scattered Iury and her vpstart groomes,

Winning from Cades to Samaria,   70

Remilia greets thee with a kinde salute

And for a present to thy mightinesse,

Giues thee a Globe folded within a ship,

As King on earth and Lord of all the Seas,

57: Aluida / DEFG(5); Aluia ABC; ALVIDA Dyce
58: bringing / CDG(3-5,Dyce)Dyce; bring ABEF   See the Commentary.
65: Rasni, / DE; -- ABCF; Rasni, Dyce

With such a welcome vnto Nyniuie   75

As may thy sisters humble loue afford.

Rasni.

Sister. The title fits not thy degree,

A higher state of honour shall be thine,

The louely Trull that Mercury intrapt,

Within the curious pleasure of his tongue,   80

And she that basht the sun-god with her eyes,

Faire Semele the choyce of Venus maides,

Were not so beautious as Remilia.

Then sweeting, sister shall not serue the turne,

But Rasnis wife, his Lemmon and his loue.   85

Thou shalt like Iuno wed thyselfe to Ioue,

And fold me in the riches of thy faire,

Remilia shall be Rasnis Paramour.

For why If I be Mars for warlike deeds?

And thou bright Venus for thy cleare aspect,   90

Why should not from our loynes issue a sonne,

That might be Lord of royall soueraintie?

Of twentie worlds, if twentie worlds might be,

What saist Remilia, art thou Rasnis wife?

Remilia.

83: Remilia./ BCDF; -- EDyce; Remelia A
85, 88: Rasnis / BCDF; Rasness A; Rasni's EDyce
94: Rasnis / BCDEF; Rasnes A; Rasni's Dyce

My heart doth swell with fauour of thy thoughts,   95

The loue of Rasni maketh me as proud

As Iuno when she wore heauens Diademe. /

Thy sister borne was for thy wife by loue,   A4v

Had I the riches nature locketh vp,

To decke her darling, beautie when she smiles,   100

Rasni should prancke him in the pride of all.

Rasni.

Remilias loue is farre more either prisde,

Then Ieroboams or the worlds subdue,

Lordings ile haue my weddings sumptuous,

Made glorious with the treasures of the world,   105

Ile fetch from Albia schelues of Margarites,

And strip the Indies of their Diamonds,

And Tyre shall yeeld me tribute of her gold,

To make Remilias wedding glorious,

Ile send for all the Damosell Queenes that liue   110

Within the reach of Rasnis gouerment,

To wait as hand-maides on Remilia,

That her attendant traine may passe the troupe

That gloried Venus at her wedding day.

Creete.

101: Rasni / BCDEFG(2)Dyce; Rasin A
102: Rasni. / BCDEFG(2-5)Dyce; Rasin. A
111: Rasnis / CDEF; Rasins A; Rasnies BG(2); Rasni's Dyce
112: Remilia, / BCDF; --; EDyce; Remelia, A

Oh my Lord, not sister to thy loue,   115

Tis incest and two fowle a fact for kings,

Nature allowes no limits to such lust.

Radagon.

Presumptuous Viceroy darst thou check thy Lord,

Or twit him with the lawes that nature lowes?

Is not great Rasni aboue natures reach,   120

God vpon earth, and all his will is law?

Creet. Oh flatter not, for hatefull is his choice,

And sisters loue will blemish all his worth.

Radagon.

Doth not the brightnesse of his maiestie,

Shadow his deeds from being counted faults?   125

Rasni.

Well hast thou answered with him Radagon,

I like thee for thy learned Sophistrie,

But thou of Creet that countercheckst thy King,

Packe hence in exile, giue Radagon thy Crowne.

119: lowes?(to allowe, or to praise) / EF; --, A; lowes, BDG(2,5, Dyce);
     loue? CG(4); loves? Dyce See the Commentary.
120: Rasni / BCDEFG(2-5)Dyce; Rasin A
121: law? / BCDEFDyce; --. A
125: faults? / BCDEFDyce; --. A
126: Rasni / BCDEFG(2)Dyce; Rasin A
126: Radagon / --; F; Radon, ABCD; Radon; E; Radagon, Dyce
126: with him / FG(Dyce); within ABCDE
129: giue Radagon thy Crowne, / CDG(3-5,Dyce); Radagon the Crowne, AF; giue
     Radagon, thy Crowne. BG(2); ⌐give⌐ Radagon thy crowne. -E; giue
     Radagon thy crown. Dyce.

Be thou Vicegerent of his royaltie.   130

And faile me not in what my thoughts may please,

For from a beggar haue I brought thee vp,

And gracst thee with the honour of a Crowne, /

Ye quandam king, what feed ye on delaies?   Bl

Creete.

Better no king then Viceroy vnder him   135

That hath no vertue to maintaine his Crowne.

Rasni.

Remilia, what faire dames be those that wait

Attendant on thy matchlesse royaltie?

Remilia.

Tis Aluida, the faire wife to the king of Paphlagonia.

Rasni. Trust me she is faire thou hast Paphlagon a Iewell,   140

To fold thee in so bright a sweetings armes.

Radagon. Like you her my Lord?

Rasni. What if I do Radagon?

Radagon.

Why then she is yours my Lord, for marriage

Makes no exception, where Rasni doth command.   145

Paphla. Ill doest thou counsel him to fancy wiues.

Rada. Wife or not wife, what so he likes is his.

130: thou / EFG(Dyce)Dyce; thee ABCD
137: Remilia, / EFDyce; Remilias, ABCD
139: Aluida / BCDE; --, F; Aluia, A; ALVIDA Dyce
140: thou hast / BCDG(2-5); thast, AF; T'hast E; th'ast Dyce

Rasni.

Well answered Radagon thou art for me,

Feed thou mine humour, and be still a king.

Lords go in tryumph of my happie loues,   150

And for to feast vs after all our broyles,

Frolicke and reuell it in Niniuie.

Whatsoeuer befitteth your conceited thoughts,

Or good or ill, loue or not loue my boyes,

In loue or what may satisfie your lust,   155

Act it my Lords, for no man dare say no.

Divisum imperium Cum Ioue nunc teneo.

                              Exeunt.

_⌐ I, ii ⌐_

Enters brought in by an Angell Oseas, the Prophet, and let downe

ouer the Stage in a Throne.   160

Angell.

Amaze not man of God, if in the spirit

Th'art brought from Iewry vnto Niniuie,

So was Elias wrapt within a storme,

And set vpon mount Carmell by the Lord,

For thou hast preacht long to the stubborne Iewes,   165

Whose flintie hearts haue felt no sweet remorse,

157: Divisum / BCDEFG(Dyce)Dyce; Denesum A See the Commentary.
159: Oseas, / -- ABCDEFDyce
159: let / CG(3,4,Dyce); set ABDEF
164: Carmell / DEFG(5,Dyce); Carnell AB; Calue CG(3,4); Carmel Dyce
    See the Commentary.

But lightly valuing all the threats of God,

Haue still perseuerd in their wickednesse. /

Loe I haue brought thee vnto <u>Niniuie</u>,

The rich and royall Citie of the world,   170

Pampred in wealth, and ouergrowne with pride,

As <u>Sodome</u> and <u>Gomorrha</u> full of sin,

The Lord lookes downe, and cannot see one good,

Not one that couets to obey his will,

But wicked all, from Cradle to the Cruch.   175

Note then <u>Oseas</u> all their greeuous sinnes,

And see the wrath of God that paies reuenge.

And when the ripenesse of their sin is full,

And thou hast written all their wicked through,

Ile carry thee to <u>Iewry</u> backe againe,   180

And seate thee in the great <u>Ierusalem</u>,

There shalt thou publish in her open streetes,

That God sends downe his hatefull wrath for sin,

On such as neuer heard his Prophets speake,

Much more will he inflict a world of plagues,   185

On such as heare the sweetnesse of his voice,

And yet obey not what his Prophets speake,

Sit thee <u>Oseas</u> pondring in the spirit,

The mightinesse of these fond people sinnes.

<u>Oseas</u>. The will of the Lord be done.   190

<u>Exit</u> <u>Angell</u>.

Enters the Clowne and his crew of Ruffians,

  to go to drinke.

/¯First¯7 Ruffian. Come on Smyth, thou shalt be one

of the Crew, because thou knowst where the best Ale   195

in Town is.

Adam.

Come on, in faith my colts I haue left my Master

striking of a heat, and stole away because I would

keep you company.

Clowne.

Why what shall we haue this paltrie Smith with vs? /   200

Adam.

Paltry Smith, why you in/¯carnatiue knaue, what are7   B2

you that you speak pettie tre/¯ason against the Smiths7

trade?

Clowne.

Why slaue I am a gentleman /¯of Niniuie.7   205

Adam. A Gentleman good sir, I remember /¯you well,

and al7 your progenitors, your father bare office in

our /¯town, and honest7 man he was, and in great

discredit in the parish, /¯for they bestowed7 two

192: Clowne. See the Commentary.
194: /¯First¬ Ruffian. / EDyce; Ruffian. ABCDF
197: Ādam. 7 EDyce; Smith. ABCD; Clowne. F
201: Ādam. / EDyce; Smith. ABCD; Clowne. F
201: All phrases in bracket are taken from B̲ to supplement the defective
   leaves of A̲ (B2 and B3).

squires liuings on him, the one was on ⌐working-
dayes,⌐ and then he kept the towne stage, and on
⌐holidaies they made⌐ him the Sextens man, for   210
he whipt dogs out of the ⌐church. Alas⌐ sir, your
father, why sir mee-thinks I see the Gen⌐tleman stil,
a⌐ proper youth, he was faith aged some foure and ten,
his b⌐eard Rats⌐ colour, halfe blacke halfe white,
his nose was in the ⌐highest de⌐gree of noses, it
was nose Autem glorificam, so set wit⌐h Rubies⌐ that   215
after his death it should haue bin nailed vp in Copp⌐er
Smiths⌐ hall for a monument: well sir, I was beholding
to your ⌐good fa⌐ther, for he was the first man that
euer instructed me in ⌐the my⌐sterie of a pot of Ale.
Second Ruffian.
Well said Smith, that crost him ouer the thumbs.   220
Clowne.
Villaine were it not that we go to be merry, m⌐y ra⌐pier
should presently quit thy opprobrious termes.
⌐Adam.⌐ O Peter, Peter, put vp thy sword I prithie
heartily into thy sc⌐ab⌐bard, hold in your rapier,
for though I haue not a long reach⌐er, I⌐ haue a short
hitter. Nay then gentlemen stay me, for my ch⌐oller⌐
begins to rise against him, for marke the words of a   225

220: Second Ruffian. / E; 2. ABCD; Second Ruf. F; SECOND RUFF. Dyce
223: ⌐ Adam. ⌐ EDyce; omitted. ABD; Smith. C; ⌐ Clowne. ⌐ F;

paltry Sm⌐īth,⌐ Oh horrible sentence, thou hast in

these words I will stand t⌐o it,⌐ libelled against all

the sound horses, whole horses, sore hors⌐es,⌐ Coursers,

Curtalls, Iades, Cuts, Hachneies, and Mares, Whe⌐re⌐

Vpon my friend, in their defence, I guie thee this

curse, thou shalt n⌐ot⌐ be worth a horse of thine owne

this seuen yeare.   230

Clowne. I prithie Smith is your occupation so

excellen⌐t?⌐

⌐ Adam. ⌐

A paltry Smith, why ile stand to it, a Smith is Lord

of the foure elements, for our yron is made of the

earth, our bellowes blows out aire, our flore holdes

fire, and our forge water. Nay sir, we reade the

Chronicles, that there was a God of our occupation. I /   235

⌐ Adam. ⌐ ⌐I, but he was⌐ a Cuckold.   B2v

⌐That was the reason sir⌐ he cold your father cousin,

paltry smith, ⌐why in this one w⌐ord thou hast defaced

their worshipfull ⌐occupation.⌐   240

⌐ Adam. ⌐ ⌐A ⌐s how?

⌐Marrie sir I will⌐ stand to it, that a Smith in his

226: words of / BG(2); words ACDEF; words, Dyce
230: Clowne./ E; I. Clcwne. ABCD; First Ruffian. F; CLOWN. Dyce
232: ⌐ Adam. ⌐⌐ EDyce; omitted ABCD;/Clowne. ⌐ F
238:⌐ Adam.⌐/ EDyce; omitted ABD; Smith. C; ⌐ Clowne. ⌐ F
242: ⌐Adam⌐// EDyce; omitted ABD; Smith. C; ⌐ Clowne.⌐ F

kinde is a Phi/sition, a Surgi/on and a Barber. For

let a Horse take a cold, or /be troubled w/ith the bots,

and we straight giue him a potion or /a Purgation, in   245

such/ physicall maner that he mends straight, if /he

haue ou/tward diseases, as the spavin, splent, ring-

bone, /windgall o/r fashion, or sir a galled backe, we

let him blood and clap /a plaist/er to him with a

pestilence, that mends him with a ve/rie ven/geance,

now if his mane grow out of order, and he haue /any   250

rebe/llious haires, we straight to our sheeres and

trim him /with/ what cut it please vs, picke his

eares and make him neat, /Marry/ indeed sir, we are

slouens for one thing, we neuer vse /any/ musk-balls

to wash him with, and the reason is sir, because /he   255

c/an woe without kissing.

Clowne. Well sirrha, leaue off these praisers of a Smyth,

/and b/ring vs to the best Ale in the Towne.

/ Adam. / /...No/w sir I haue a feate aboue all the Smythes

in Niniuie, for sir / I / am a Philosopher that can dispute

of the nature of Ale, for /ma/rke you sir, a pot of Ale

consists of foure parts, Imprimis the /Al/e, the Toast,

the Ginger, and the Nutmeg.   260

247: spavin, / EG(Dyce)Dyce; spuing, ABF; spauing DG(5)
258: / Adam. / / EDyce; omitted ABD; Smith. C; / Clowne./ F

Clowne. Excellent.

⌐ Adam. ⌐ (Th)e Ale is a restoratiue, bread is a binder, marke
you sir two excellent points in phisicke, the Ginger,
oh ware of that, the philosophers haue written of the
nature of ginger, tis expullsitiue in two degree, you
shal here the sentence of Galen, it wil make a man   265
belch, cough, and fart, and it is a great comfort to
the hart, a proper poesie I promise you, but now to
the noble vertue of the Nutmeg, it is saith one Ballad
I think an English Roman was the authour, an vnderlayer
to the braines, for when the Ale giues a buffet to   270
the head, oh the Nutmeg that keeps him for a while
in temper. Thus you see the discription of the vertue
of a pot of Ale, now sir /
to put my physical precepts in practise f/ollow   B3
me, but afore I s/tep any further.   275

Clowne.

Whats the matter now?

⌐ Adam. ⌐

Why seeing I haue prouided the Ale, who is /the
puruaor for th/e wenches? for masters take this of
me, a cup /of Ale without a/ wench, why alasse tis

261: ⌐ Adam. ⌐ / E; omitted ABCD; ⌐ Clowne. ⌐ F; ADAM. Dyce
267: and it is / CG(3,4); and is ABDEFDyce
272: for a while / CDEFDyce; for while ABG(2)
277: ⌐ Adam. ⌐ / E; omitted ABCD; ⌐ Clowne. ⌐ F; ADAM. Dyce

like an egge without salt, o/r a red he/rring without

mustard.   280

/ Clowne. /

Lead vs to the Ale, weele haue wenches inough I

w/arrent/ thee.

Oseas.

Iniquitie seekes out companions still,

And mortall men are armed to do ill:

London looke on, this matter nips thee neere,

Leaue off thy ryot, pride and sumptuous cheere.   285

Spend lesse at boord, and spare not at the doore,

But aide the infant, and releeue the poore:

Else seeking mercy being mercilesse,

Thou be adiudged to endlesse heauinesse.

/ I, iii /

Enter the Vsurer, / Thrasibulus, / a young Gentleman,   290

    and / Alcon, / a poore man.

Vsurer.   Come on, I am euery day troubled with these

needie companions, what newes with you, what wind brings

you hither?

281: / Clowne. / / CE; omitted ABD; / First Ruffian. / F; CLOWN. Dyce
290-291: a yoong Gentleman, and a poore man. See the Commentary.
290: Enter. / CG(3,4,Dyce)Dyce; Enters. ABDEF
290: / Thrassibulus, / a yoong Gentleman, / a yoong Gentleman, ABCD;
        Thrasybulus, E; / Thrasibulus / F; THRASIBULUS, Dyce
290: / Alcon, / a poore man. / a poore man. ABCD; a poore Man / Alcon /.
        F; Alcon. E; ALCON. Dyce
293: hither? / CFDyce; --. ABDE

Gent. Sir I hope how far foeuer you make it off, you 295
remember too well for me, that this is the day wherein
I should pay you mony that I tooke vp of you alate in
a commoditie.

Poore man. And sir, sirreuerence of your manhood and
gentrie, I haue brought home such mony as you lent me.

Vsurer. You yoong Gentleman is my mony readie? 300

Gentle. Truly sir this time was so short, the commoditie
so bad, and the promise of friends so broken, that I
could not prouide it against the day, wherefore I am
come to intreat you to stand my friend and to fauour
me with a longer time, and I will make you sufficient
consideration. 305

Vsurer

Is the winde in that doore? if thou hast my mony so
it is, I will not defer a day, an houre, a minute,
but take the forfeyt / B3v

/of the bond./

/ Gent. /

/I pray you/ sir consider that my losse was great by
the /commoditie I too/ke vp, you knowe sir I borrowed
of you fortie /pounds, whereof/ I had ten pounds in 310
money, and thirty pounds /in Lute strings/, which

300: readie? / BCDE; --. A; ready? Dyce
306: door? / CEFDyce; doore, ABD

when I came to see againe, I could get /but fiu<u>e</u>7

poundes for them, so had I sir but fifteene poundes

for /m̄y fortie:_7 In consideration of this ill bargaine,

I pray you sir /ḡiue me <u>a</u>7 month longer.   315

/V̄sur7er.

I answered thee afore not a minute, what haue I to do

how they bargain proued? I haue thy hand set to my

booke that thou receiuedst fortie pounds of me in mony.

Gent. I sir it was your deuise to colour the Statute,

but your conscience knowes what I had.   320

Poore.

Friend thou speakest Hebrew to him when th(ou) talkest

to him of conscience, for he hath as much conscience

about the forfeyt of an Obligation, as my blinde Mare

God blesse her, hath ouer a manager of Oates.

Gent. Then there is no fauour sir?   325

Vsurer.

Come to morrow to mee, and see how I will vse thee.

Gent.

No couetous Caterpillar, know, that I haue made extreme

shift rather then I would fall into the hands of such

a rauening panthar, and therefore here is the mony

and deliuer me the recognisance of my lands.   330

317: proued? / EF; -- ABC<u>D</u>; proved? <u>Dyce</u>
319: <u>omitted</u> / B̄C̄Ḏ; that, AEFDyce

Vsurer.

What a spight is this, hath sped of his Crownes, if he

had mist but one halfe houre, what a goodly Farme had

I gotten for fortie pounds, well tis my cursed fortune,

Oh haue I no shift to make him forfeit his recognisance?   335

Gent.

Come sir will you dispatch and tell your mony?

Strikes 4 aclocke.

Vsurer.

Stay, what is this a clocke foure, let me see, to be

paid between the houres of three and foure in the

afternoone, this goes right for me, you sir, heare

you not the clocke, and haue you not a counterpaine   340

of your Obligation? the houre is past, it was to be

paid betweene three and foure, and now clocke hath

strooken /

foure, I will receiue none, Ile stand to the forfeyt   B4

of the recognisance.

Gent. Why sir, I hope you do but iest, why tis but   345

foure, and will you for a minute take forfeyt of my

bond? if it were so sir, I was here before foure.

Vsurer.

335: recognisance? / CF; --. ABDE; --; Dyce
336: mony? / BCEFDyce; --. AD
341: Obligation? / C; --, AB; --: D; obligation? EFDyce
346: bond? / BCFDyce; --, ADE

Why didst thou not tender thy mony then? if I offer
thee iniury take the law of me, complaine to the
Iudge, I will receiue no mony. 350

Poore.

Well sir, I hope you will stand my good maister for
my Cow, I borrowed thirtie shillings on her, and for
that I haue paid you 18. pence a weeke, and for her
meate you haue had her milke, and I tell you sir, she
giues a goodly soape: now sir here is your money. 355

Vsurer.

Hang beggarly knaue, commest to me for a Cow? did I
not bind her bought and sold for a penny, and was not
thy day to haue paid yesterday? thou getst no Cow at
my hand.

Poore.

No Cow sir, alasse that word no Cow, goes as cold to
my heart as a draught of small drinke in a frostie 360
morning. No Cow sir, why alasse, alasse, M. Vsurer,
what shall become of me my wife, and my poore childe?

Vsurer.

Thou getst no Cow of me knaue, I cannot stand prating
with you, I must be gone.

Poore.

356: Cow? / EFDyce; --, ABCD
358: yesterday? / BCDEFDyce; -- A

Nay but heare you M. Vsurer, no Cow, why sir heres 365
your thirtie shillings, I haue paid you 18. pence a
weeke, and therefore there is a reason 1 should haue
my Cow.

Vsurer.

What pratest thou, haue I not answered thee thy day is
broken?

Poore.

Why sir alasse, my Cow is a Common-wealth to me, for
first sir, she allowes me, my wife and sonne, for to 370
banket our selues withal, Butter, Cheese, Whay, Curds,
Creame, sod mild, raw-mile, sower-milke, sweete-milk,
and butter-milke, besides sir, she saued me euery
yeare a peny in Almanackes, for she was as good to
me as a Prognostication, if she had but set vp her 375
tayle and haue gallpt about the meade, my litle boy
was able to say, oh father there will be a storme,
her verie taile was a Kalander to me, and now to loose
my cow, alas M. Vsurer take pittie vpon me. /

Vsurer.

I haue other matters to talke on, farwell fellowes. B4v

Gent.

Why but thou couetous churle, wilt thou not receiue 380
thy mony and deliuer me my recognisance?

Vsurer.

Ile deliuer thee none, if I haue wronged thee, seeke

thy mends at the law.   /Exit.

Gent.

And so I will insatiable pesant.

Poore.

And sir, rather then I will put vp this word no Cow,

I will laie my wiues best gowne to pauwne, I tell   385

you sir, when the slaue vttered this word no Cow,

it strooke to my heart, for my wife shall neuer haue

one so fit for her turne againe, for indeed sir, she

is a woman that hath her twidling strings broke.

Gent.

What meanest thou by that fellow?   390

Poore.

Marry sir, sirreuerence of your manhood, she breakes

behinde, and indeed sir, when she sat milking of her

Cow and let a fart, my other Cowes would start at the

noyse, and kick downe the milke and away, but this Cow

sir the gentlest Cow, my wife might blow whilst she

bust, and hauing such conditions, shall the   395

Vsurer come vpon me with no Cow? Nay sir, before

I pocket vp this word no Cow, my wiues gowne goes to

the Lawyer, why alasse sir tis as ill a word to me,

as no Crowne to a King.

_____

383: ⌐ Exit. / EFDyce; omitted. ABCD
396: no Cow? / BCD; --: A; '--'? EF; no cow? Dyce

Gent.

Well fellow, go with me, and ile helpe thee to a   400

Lawyer.

Poore.

Marry and I will sir: No Cow, well the world goes

hard.   Exeunt.

                        Oseas.

Oseas.

Where hateful vsurie   405

Is counted husbandrie,

Where mercilesse men rob the poore,

And the needie are thrust out of doore.

Where gaine is held for conscience,

And mens pleasures are all on pence,   410

Where yong Gentlemen forfeit their lands,

Through riot, into the Vsurers hands:

Where pouertie is despisde and pity banished

And mercy indeed vtterly vanished. /

Where men esteeme more of money then of God.   415   Cl

Let that land looke to feele his wrathfull rod.

For there is no sin more odious in his sight,

Then where vsurie defraudes the poore of his right.

London take heed, these sinnes abound in thee:

The poore complaine, the widowes wronged bee.   420

410: pleasures are / G(Dyce)Dyce; pleasures is ABDEF; pleasure is CG(4)

The Gentlemen by subtiltie are spoilde,

The plough-men loose the crop for which they toild.

Sin raignes in thee o London euery houre,

Repent and tempt not thus the heauenly power.

/ II, i 7

    Enters Remilia, with a traine of Ladies   425

            in all royaltie.

Remilia.

Faire Queenes, yet handmaids vnto Rasnies loue,

Tell me, is not my state as glorious

As Iunoes pomp, when tyred with heauens despoile,

Clad in her vestments, spotted all with starres,   430

She crost the siluer path vnto her Ioue,

Is not Remilia far more beautious,

Rich'd with the pride of natures excellence,

Then Venus in the brightest of her shine?

My haires, surpasse they not Apollos locks?   435

Are not my Tresses curled with such art,

As loue delights to hide him in their faire?

Doth not mine eyne shine like the morning lampe

427: Rasnies / CG(3,4); Rasnes ABD; Rasnis EF; Rasni's Dyce
430: Clad in her vestments, spotted all with starres, / CEF; Clad in her
    vestments, spotted all with starres, ABD
432: Remilia / EFDyce; Remilias ABCD
433: Rich'd / Dyce; Rich BCDG(2,5); Richt AEF
433: excellence, / G(Dyce)Dyce; --? A; --; DFG(5); excellencie? BG(2); --,
    CEG(3,4)
434: shine? / BCG(2,4,Dyce)Dyce; -- AF; --, DG(5)
435: locks? / DEFDyce; -- ABC

That tels Aurora when her loue will come?

Haue I not stolne the beautie of the heauens,   440

And plac'st it on the feature of my face?

Can any Goddesse make compare with me?

Or match her with the faire Remilia?

Alvuida.

The beauties that proud Paris saw from Troy

Mustring in Ida for the golden ball,   445

Were not so gorgeous as Remilia.

Remilia.

I haue trickt my tramels vp with richest balme,

And made my perfumes of the purest Myrre:

The pretious drugs that Aegypts wealth affords, /

The costly paintings fetcht from curious Tyre,   450   Clv

Haue mended in my face what nature mist.

Am I not the earths wonder in my lookes?

Alui.

The wonder of the earth and pride of heauen.

Remilia.

Looke Aluida a haire stands not amisse,

For womens locks are tramels of conceipt,   455

Which do intangle loue for all his wiles.

Aluid.

439: Aurora / CDEFG(3-5,Dyce)Dyce; Aurera ABG(2)
444: from / BDFG(2-5,Dyce)Dyce; fro ACE

Madam, vnlesse you coy it trick and trim,

And plaie the ciuill wanton ere you yeeld,

Smiting disdaine of pleasures with your tongue,

Patting your princely Rasni on the cheeke,   460

When he presumes to kisse without consent:

You marre the market, beautie nought auiles.

You must be proud, for pleasures hardly got,

Are sweete, if once attainde.

Remilia.

Faire Aluida,   465

They counsell makes Remilia passing wise.

Suppose that thou weart Rasnies mightinesse,

And I Remilia Prince of excellence.

Aluida.

I would be maister then of loue and thee.

Remil.

Of loue and me? Proud and disdainful king,   470

Dar'st thou presume to touch a Deitie,

Before she grace thee with a yeelding smile?

Alvida.

Tut my Remilia, be not thou so coy,

Say nay, and take it.

Remilia.

467: Rasnies / CG(3,4); Rasnes ABD; Rasnis EF; Rasni's Dyce
470: me? / B; --. AC; --'? E; --; D; --:F; --! Dyce

Carelesse and vnkinde,   475

Talkes Rasni to Remilia in such sort

As if I did enioy a humane forme?

Looke on thy Loue, behold mine eyes diuine,

And dar'st thou twit me with a womans fault?

Ah Rasni thou art rash to iudge of me,   480

I tell thee Flora oft hath woode my lips,

To lend a Rose to beautifie her spring,

The sea-Nymphs fetch their lillies from my cheeks.

Then thou vnkind, and hereon would I weepe.

Alui.

And here would Aluida resigne her charge, /   485

For were I but in thought Th'Assirian King,   C2

I needs must quiet thy teares, with kisses sweete,

And craue a pardon with a friendly touch,

You know it Madam though I teach it not,

The touch I meane, you smile when as you think it.   490

Remi.

How am I pleas'd to hear thy pritty prate,

According to the humor of my minde?

Ah Nymphs, who fairer then Remilia?

The gentle winds haue woode me with their sighes,

486: Th'Assirian / th'Assirian EDyce; Th'assirian ABCD
490: it. / EFG(Dyce); il. AB; ill. CDG(3-5)

The frowning aire hath cleerde when I did smile,   495

And when I tract vpon the tender grasse,

Loue that makes warme the center of the earth,

Lift vp his crest to kisse Remelias foote,

Iuno still entertaines her amorous Ioue,

With new delights, for feare he looke on me,   500

The Phoenix feathers are become my Fanne,

For I am beauties Phoenix in this world.

Shut close these Curtaines straight and shadow me,

For feare Apollo spie me in his walkes,

And scorne all eyes, to see Remilias eyes.   505

Nymphes, eunucks, sing, for Mauors draweth nigh,

Hide me in Closure, let him long to looke,

For were a Goddesse fairer then am I,

Ile scale the heauens to pull her from the place.

    They draw the Curtaines and Musicke   510

        plaies.

Aluida.

Beleeue me, though she say that she is fairest,

I thinke my peny siluer by her leaue.

    Enter Rasni with his Lords in pomp, who makes a

      ward about him, with him the Magi   515

        in great pompe.

506: eunuchs, / EG(Dyce)Dyce; Knanck, ABCD; Enuchs, F

Rasni.

Magi for loue of Rasni by your Art,

By Magicke frame an Arbour out of hand,

For faire Remilia to desport her in.

Meane-while, I will bethinke me on further pomp.   520

Exit. /

The Magi with their rods beate the Cloud, and from   C2v

    vnder the same riseth a braue Arbour, the King

returned in an other sute while the Trumpettes sounde.   525

Rasni.

Blest be ye men of Art that grace me thus,

And blessed be this day where Himen hies,

To ioyne in vnion pride of heauen and earth.

    Lightning and thunder where with Remilia

           is strooken.   530

What wondrous threatning noyse is this I heare?

What flashing lightnings trouble our delights?

When I draw neare Remilias royal Tent,

I waking, dreame of sorrow and mishap.

Radagon.

Dread not O King, at ordinary chance,   535

These are but common exaltations,

Drawne from the earth, in substance hote and drie,

526: men / DEFG(5,Dyce); man ABC
536: exaltations, / CG(4); exalations, A; exalitations BDG(2,5); exhalations, Dyce

Or moist and thicke, or Meteors combust,

Matters and causes incident to time,

Inkindled in the firie region first,   540

Tut be not now a Romane Augurer,

Approach the Tent, looke on Remilia.

Rasni.

Thou hast confirmd my doubts kinde Radagon.

Now ope ye foldes where Queene of fauour sits,

Carrying a Net within her curled locks,   545

Wherein the Graces are entangled oft:

Ope like th' imperiall gates where Phoebus sits,

When as he meanes to wooe his Clitia.

Necternall Cares, ye blemishers of blisse,

Cloud not mine eyes whilst I behold her face.   550

Remilia my delight, she answereth not.

He drawes the Curtaines and findes her stroken

            with Thunder, blacke.

How pale? as if bereau'd in fatall meedes,

The balmy breath hath left her bosome quite, /   555

My Hesperus by cloudie death is blent,   C3

Villaines away, fetch Sirropes of the Inde,

Fetch Balsomo the kind preserue of life,

Fetch wine of Greece, fetch oiles, fetch herbes,

            fetch all

541: Augurer, / DFG(5); --: E; Angurer, ABC; augurer: Dyce

To fetch her life, or I will faint and die.   560

They bring in all these and offer, nought preuailes.

Herbes, Oyles of Inde, alasse there nought preuailes.

Shut are the day-bright eyes, that made me see,

Lockt are the Iems of ioy in dens of death,

Yet triumph I on fate, and he on her.   565

Malicious mistresse of inconstancie,

Damd be thy name, that hast obscur'd my ioy,

Kings, Viceroyes, Princes, reare a royall tombe

For my Remilia, beare her from my sight,

Whilst I in teares, weepe for Remilia.   570

                    They beare her out.

Radagon.

What makes Rasni moodie? Losse of one?

As if no more were left so faire as she?

Behold a daintie minion for the nonce,

Faire Aluida the Paphlagonian Queene,   575

Wooe her, and leaue this weeping for the dead.

Ras.

What wooe my subiects wife that honoreth me?

Rad.

Tut kings this meum tuum should not know.

Is she not faire? Is not her husband hence?

Holt, take her at the hands of Radagon.   580

572: one? / BCDFDyce; --, E; oue? A

A prittie peate to driue your mourne away.

Rasni.

She smiles on me, I see she is mine owne.

Wilt thou be Rasnies royall Paramour?

Rad.

She blushing yeelds concent, make no dispute:

The King is sad, and must be gladded straight.   585

Let Paphlagonian King go mourne mean-while.

    He thrusts the King out, and so they exeunt.

Oseas.

Pride hath his iudgement, London looke about,

Tis not inough in show to be deuout,

A Furie now from heauen to lands vnknowne,   590

Hath made the Prophet speake, not to his owne, /

Flie wantons flie, this pride and vaine attire,   C3v

The seales to set your tender hearts on fire.

Be faithfull in the promise you haue past,

Else God will plague and punish at the last.   595

When lust is hid in shroude of wretched life,

When craft doth dwell in bed of married wife.

Marke but the Prophets, we that shortly showes,

After death expect for many woes.

   ⌜ II, ii ⌝

583: Rasnies / DG(5); rasnies G(4); Rasnes ABC; Rasni's Dyce
587: thrusts / BCFDyce; thrust A; thrust(s) DEG(5)
587: exeunt./ BG(2)Dyce; Exeant. ACDEF
599: expect / CDEDyce; exspect A; expects BF

Enters ⌐ Alcon, ⌐ the poore man and ⌐ Thrasibulus, ⌐   600

the Gentleman, with their Lawier.

Gent.

I need not sir discourse vnto you the dutie of Lawiers

in tendring the right cause of their Clients, nor the

conscience you are tied vnto by higher command.

Therefore suffise the Vsurer hath done me wrong, you

know the Case, and good sir, I haue strained my selfe   605

to giue you your fees.

Lawier.

Sir if I should any way neglect so manifest a truth,

I were to be accused of open periury, for the case

is euident.

Poore.

And truly sir, for my case, if you helpe me not

for my matter, why sir, I and my wife are quite vndone,

I want my mease of milke when I goe to worke, and my   610

boy his bread and butter when he goes to schoole,

Master Lawier pitie me, for surely sir, I was faine

to laie my wiues best gowne to pawne for your fees,

when I lookt vpon it sir, and saw how hansomly it was

600: ⌐ Alcon, ⌐the poore man / the poore man ABCD; ALCON Dyce; Alcon E;
      a poore Man ⌐ Alcon ⌐ F
600: ⌐ Thrasibulus, ⌐ the Gentleman, / Thrasybulus, a yoong Gentleman E;
      ⌐ Thrasibulus ⌐, F; THRASIBULUS, Dyce; the gentleman, BCD; the
      Gentlemau, A

dawbed with statute lace, and what a faire mockado 615

Cape it had, and then thought how hansomely it became

my wife, truly sir my heart is made of butter, it

melts at the least persecution, I fell on weeping, but

when I thought on the words the Vsurer gaue me, no Cow:

then sir, I would haue stript her into her smocke,

but I would make him deliuer my Cow ere I had done, 620

therefore good M. Lawier stand my friend.

Lawier.

Trust me father, I will do for thee as much as for

my selfe.

Poore.

Are you married sir?

Lawier.

I marry and am I father. 625

Poore.

Then goods Benison light on you and your good wife, /

and send her that she be neuer troubled with my wiues Cl4

disease.

Lawier.

Why whats thy wiues disease?

Poore.

Truly sir, she hath two open faults, and one priuie

fault, sir the first is, she is too eloquent for a

poore man, and hath her words of Art, for she will 630

call me Rascall, Rogue, Runnagate, Varlet, Vagabond,

Slaue, and Knaue. Why alasse sir, and these be but
holi-day tearmes, but if you heard her working-day
words, in faith sir they be ratlers like thunder sir,
for after the dewe followes a storme, for then am I
sure either to be well buffetted, my face scratcht,
or my head broken, and therefore good M. Lawyer on   635
my knees I ask it, let me not go home again to my
wife, with this word, No Cow: for then shee will
exercise her two faults vpon me with all extremitie.

Lawier.

Feare not man, but what is they wiues priuy fault?   640

Poore.

Truly sir, thats a thing of nothing, alasse she
indeed sirreuerence of your mastership, doth vse
to breake winde in her sleepe. Oh sir, here comes
the Iudge, and the old Caitife the Vsurer.

Enters the Iudge, the Vsurer, and his attendants.   645

Vsurer.

Sir here is fortie angels for you, and if at any time
you want a hundreth pound or two, tis readie at your
command, or the feeding of three or foure fat bullocks:
whereas these needie slaues can reward with nothing
but a cap and a knee, and therefore I pray you sir

632: and knaue / BCDG(2-5); knaue AEF; knave Dyce

fauour my case.   650

Iudge.

Fear not sir, Ile do what I can for you.

Vsurer.

What maister Lawier what make you here, mine

aduersary for these Clients?

Lawier.

So it changeth now sir.

Vsurer.

I know you know the old Prouerbe, He is not wise,   655

that is not wise for himselfe. I would not be

disgracst in this action, therefore here is twentie

angeles say nothing in the matter, and what you say,

say to no purpose, for the Iudge is my friend.

Lawier.

Let me alone, Ile fit your purpose.

Iudge.

Come, where are these fellowes that are the   660

plaintifes, what can they say against this honest

Citizen our neighbour, a man of good report amongst

all men? /

Poore.

Truly M. Iudge, he is a man much spoken off, marry   C4v

euery mans cries are against him, and especially

we, and therefore I thinke we haue brought our Lawier   665

to touch him with as much law as will fetch his landes

and my Cowe, with a pestilence.

Gent.

Sir, I am the other plaintife and this is my
Councellour, I beseech your honour be fauourable to
me in equitie.

Iudge.

Oh Signor Mizaldo, what can you say in this   670
Gentlemans behalfe?

Lawier.

Faith sir, as yet litle good, sir tell you your owne
case to the Iudge, for I haue so many matters in my
head, that I haue almost forgotten it.

Gent.

Is the winde in that doore? why then my Lord thus,   675
I took vp of this cursed Vsurer, for so I may well
tearme him, a commoditie of fortie poundes, whereof I
receiued ten pounde in mony, and thirtie pound in Lute-
strings, whereof I could by great friendship make but
fiue pounds: for the assurance of this badde commoditie,
I bound him my land in recognisance, I came at my   680
day and tendred him his mony and he would not take
it, for the redresse of my open wrong, I craue but
iustice.

Iudge.

_____

675: doore? / BCEF; --; D; doore A; door? Dyce

What say you to this sir?

<u>Vsurer.</u>

That first he had no Lute-strings of me, for looke
you sir, I haue his owne hand to my booke for the
receit of fortie pound.   685

<u>Gent.</u>

That was sir, but a deuise of him to colour the
Statute.

<u>Iudge.</u>

Well he hath thine owne hand, and we can craue no
more law, but now sir, he saies his money was tendred
at the day and houre.   690

<u>Vsurer.</u>

This is manifest contrary sir, and on that I will
depose, for here is the obligation, to be paide
betweene three and foure in the after-noone, and the
Clocke strooke foure before he offered it, and the
words be betweene three and foure, therefore to be
tendred before foure.   695

<u>Gent.</u>

Sir, I was there before foure, and he held me with
brabling till the Clock strooke, and then for the
breach of a minute he refused my money, and kept the
recognisance of my land for so /

698: kept / <u>DEFG</u>(5, <u>Dyce</u>)<u>Dyce</u>; keepe <u>ABC</u>

small a trifle: good <u>Signor Mizaldo</u> speak what is law,   D1

you haue your fee, you haue heard what the case is,   700

and therefore do me iustice and right, I am a yoong

Gentleman and speake for my patrimony.

<u>Lawier.</u>

Faith sir, the Case is altered, you told me it before

in an other maner, the law goes quite against you,

and therefore you must pleade to the Iudge for   705

fauour.

<u>Gent.</u>

O execrable bribery.

<u>Poore.</u>

Faith sir Iudge, I pray you let me be the Gentlemans

Counsellour, for I can say thus much in his defence,

that the Vsurers Clocke is the swiftest Clock in all

the Towne, tis sir like a womans tongue, it goes euer

halfe an houre before the time, for when we were gone   710

from him, other Clocks in the Towne strooke foure.

<u>Iudge.</u>

Hold thy prating fellow, and you yoong Gentleman,

this is my ward, looke better another time both to

your bargains and to the paiments, for I must giue

flat sentence against you, that for default of   715

tendering the mony betweene the houres, you haue

forfeited your recognisance, and he to haue the land.

Gent.

O inspeakable iniustice.

Poore.

O monstrous, miserable, moth-eaten Iudge.

Iudge. Now you fellow, what haue you to say for your

matter?   720

Poore.

Maister Lawier, I laid my wiues gowne to pawne for

your fees, I pray you to this geere.

Lawier.

Alasse poore man, thy matter is out of my hand, and

therefore I pray thee tell it thy selfe.   725

Poore.

I hold my Cap to a noble, that the Vsurer hath giuen

him some gold, and he chawing it in his mouth, hath

got and toothache that he cannot speake.

Iudge.

Well sirrha, I must be short, and therefore say on.

Poore.

Maister Iudge, I borrowed of t his man thirtie   730

shillings, for which I left him in pawne my good Cow,

the bargaine was, he should haue eighteene pence a

weeke and the Cows milk for vsurie: Now sir, as soone

as I had gotten the mony, I brought it him, and broke

730: Maister / Master G(5,Dyce)Dyce; O Maister G(4); M. Maister A but a day, and for that he refused his mony and /

keeps my Cow sir.

Iudge.

Why thou hast giuen sentence against thy selfe, for

in breaking thy day thou hast lost thy Cow.

Poore.

Master Lawier now for my ten shillings.

Lawier.

Faith poore man, thy Case is so bad I shalt but

speak against thee. 740

Poore.

Twere good then I should haue my ten shillings again.

Lawier.

Tis my fee fellow for comming, wouldst thou haue

me come for nothing?

Poore.

Why then am I like to goe home, not onely with no

Cow, but no gowne, this geere goes hard. 745

Iudge.

Well you haue heard what fauour I can shew you, I

must do iustice, come M. Mizaldo and you sir, go

home with me to dinner.

Poore.

Why but M. Iudge no Cow, and M. Lawier no gowne,

Then must I cleane run out of the Towne.   750

    / Exeunt Iudge, Lawier, Vsurer, and Attendants. /

How cheere you gentleman, you crie no lands too, the

Iudge hath made you a knight for a gentleman, hath

dubd you sir Iohn lackland.

Gent.

O miserable time wherein gold is aboue God.

Poore.

Fear not man, I haue yet a fetch to get thy landes

and my Cow againe, for I haue a sonne in the Court   755

that is either a king or a kings fellow, and to him

will I go and complaine on the Iudge and the Vsurer

both.

Gent.

And I will go with thee and intreat him for my Case.

Poore.

But how shall I go home to my wife, when I shall   760

haue nothing to say vnto her, but no Cow?

Alasse sir my wiues faults will fall vpon me.

Gent.

Feare not, lets go, Ile quiet her shalt see.

                           Exeunt.

Oseas.

750-751: / Exeunt Iudge, Lawier, Vsurer, and Attendants. / F; omitted
ABCD; / Exeunt Judge attended, Lawyer, and Vsurer. / E; Exeunt
Judge, Lawyer, and Usurer. Dyce

Flie Iudges flie, corruption in your Court,   765

The Iudge of truth, hath made your iudgement short.

Looke so to iudge that at the latter day,

Ye be not iudg'd with those that wend astray.

Who passeth iudgement for his priuate gaine.

He well may iudge, he is adiudg'd to paine. /   770

⌜ II, iii ⌝

Enters ⌜ Adam, ⌝ the Clowne and all his crew drunke.   D2

Adam.

Farewell gentle Tapster, maisters as good as euer

was tapt, looke to your feete, for the Ale is strong,

well farewell gentle Tapster.

I. Ruffian.

Why sirrha slaue, by heauens maker, thinkest thou   775

the wench loues thee best because she laught on thee,

giue me but such an other word, and I will throw the

pot at thy head.

Adam.

Spill no drinke, spill no drinke, the Ale is good,

Ile tel you what, Ale is Ale, and so Ile commend me

to you with heartie commendations, farewell gentle   780

Tapster.

771: ⌜ Adam, ⌝ / Dyce; omitted ABCDEF See the Commentary.
776: Ioues / BCDG(2-5,Dyce); loues EDyce; loue AF
772, 778: Adam./ E; Clowne. ABCDF; ADAM. Dyce

2. Ruffian.

Why wherefore peasant scornst thou that the wench

should loue me, looke but on her, and il thrust my

dagger in thy bosome.

I. Ruffian.

Well sirrha well, thart as thart, and so ile take

thee.

2. Ruffian.

Why what am I?   785

I. Ruffian.

Why what thou wilt, a slaue.

2. Ruffian.

Then take that villaine, and learne how thou vse me

another time.

1. Ruffian.

Oh I am slaine.

2. Ruffian.

Thats all one to me, I care not, now wil I in to my

wench and call for a fresh pot.   790

Adam.

781, 785, 787: 2. Ruffian. / Second Ruf. E; 2. ABCD; RUFFIAN. Dyce;
     Sec. Ruff. F

784: thee. / BCEFG(2)Dyce; .. AD

786, 788: I. Ruffian. / 1. RUFFIAN Dyce; I. ABCD; First Ruf. E; First
     Ruff. F

791, 808, 813, 815, 821, 826, 831, 836, 851, 854: Adam./ E; ADAM. Dyce;
     Clowne. ABCDF

Nay but heare ye, take me with ye, for the Ale is Ale,

cut a fresh toast Tapster, fil me a pot here is mony,

I am no beggar, Ile follow thee as long as the Ale

lasts: a pestilence on the blocks for me, for I might

haue had a fall, wel if we shal haue no Ale ile sit   795

me downe, and so farwell gentle Tapster.

   Here he fals ouer the dead man.

Enters Rasni, the King, Aluida, the King of Cilicia,

   with other attendants.

Rasni.

What slaughtred wretch lies bleeding here his last?

So neare the royall pallacie of the King.   800

Search out if any one be biding nie,

That can discourse the maner of his death,

Seate thee faire Aluida, the faire of faires,

Let not the obiect once offend thine eyes,

Lord.

Heres one sits here asleepe my Lord.   805

Rasni.

Wake him and make enquiry of this thing. /

Lord.

Sirrha you, hearest thou fellow?   D2v

797: ⌐ Rasni, ⌐ the King / Dyce; the King ABCDEF
797-798: omitted / FDyce; and of Paphlagonia, ABCDE See the Commentary.
798: attendants. / CDEFDyce; attendant. AB
804: obiect / EFDyce; otrict ABCD
805: Lord. / BCEFG(2,3, Dyce); --, AD

Adam.

If you will fill a fresh pot heares a peny, or else
farewell gentle Tapster.

Lord.

He is drunke my Lord.   810

Rasni.

Welle sport with him that <u>Aluida</u> may laugh.

Lord.

Sirrha thou fellow, thou must come to the King.

Adam.

I will not do a stroke of worke to day, for the Ale
is good Ale, and you can aske but a peny for a pot,
no more by the statute.   815

Lord.

Villaine, heres the King, thou must come to him.

Adam.

The King come to an Ale-house, Tapster, fil me three
pots, wheres the King, is this he? giue me your hand
sir, as good Ale as euer was tapt, you shall drinke
while your skin cracke.

Rasni.

But herest thou fellow, who kild this man?   820

Adam.

Ile tell you sir, if you did taste of the Ale, all
<u>Niniuie</u> hath not such a cup of Ale, it floures in the
cup, sir, by my troth I spent eleuen pence beside three

rases of ginger.

Rasni.

Answer me knaue to my question, how came this man   825

slaine?

Adam.

Slain, why Ale is strong Ale, tis hufcap, I warrent

you twill make a man well, Tapster ho, for the King

a cup of ale and a fresh toast, heres two rases more.

Aluida.

Why good fellow the King talkes not of drinke, he

would haue thee tell him know this man came dead.   830

Adam.

Dead nay, I thinke I am aliue yet, and wil drink a

ful pot ere night, but here ye, if ye be the wench

that fild vs drink, why so do your office, and giue

vs a fresh pot, or if you be the Tapsters wife, why

so, wash the glasse cleane.

Aluida.

He is so drunke my Lord, theres no talking with him.   835

Adam.

Drunke, nay then wench I am not drunke,

thart a shitten queane to call me drunke, I tell thee

I am not drunke, I am a Smith I.

    Enters the Smith, the Clownes / Adam's _7 maister.   840

Lord.

Sir here comes one perhaps that can tell.

Smith.

God saue you master. /

Rasni.

Smith canst thou tell me how this man came dead?   D3

Smith.

May it please your highnesse, my man here and a crue

of them went to the ale-house, and came out so drunke

that one of them kild another, and now sir, I am   845

faine to leaue my shop and come to fetch him home.

Rasni.

Some of you carry away the dead bodie, druncken

men must haue their fits, and sirrha Smith hence with

thy man.

Smith.

Sirrha you, rise come go with me.   850

Adam.

If we shall haue a pot of Ale lets haue it, heres

mony, hold Tapster take my purse.

Smith.

Come then with me, the pot stands full in the house.

Adam.

I am for you, lets go, thart an honest Tapster, weele

drinke sixe pots ere we part.   855

                                 Exeunt.

————————————

853: Smith./ BCDEFDyce; Smith A

Rasni.

Beautious, more bright then beautie in mine eyes,

Tell me faire sweeting, wants thou any thing?

Conteind within the threefold circle of the world,

That may make Aluida liue full content.   860

Aluida.

Nothing my Lord, for all my thoughts are pleasde,

When as mine eye surfets with Rasnies sight.

Enters the King of Paphlagonia, male-content.

Rasni.

Looke how thy husband haunts our royall Courts,

How still his sight breeds melancholy stormes,   865

Oh, Aluida I am passing passionate,

And vext with wrath and anger to the death,

Mars when he held faire Venus on his knee,

And saw the limping Smith come from his forge,

Had not more deeper furrowes in his brow,   870

Then Rasni hath to see his Paphlagon.

Alui.

Content thee sweet, ile salue thy sorrow straight,

Rest but the ease of all thy thoughts on me,

And if I make not Rasni blyth againe,

Then say that womens fancies haue no shifts.   875

862: Rasnies / CG(3,4); Rasnes ABD; Rasni's Dyce
866: passing / BCDEFG(2-5)Dyce; passion A

Paphla.

Shamst thou not Rasni though thou beest a King,

To shroude adultry in thy royall seate?

Art thou arch-ruler of great Niniuie, /

Who shouldst excell in vertue as in state,   D3v

And wrongst thy friend by keeping backe his wife?   880

Haue I not battail'd in thy troupes full oft,

Gainst Aegypt, Iury, and proud Babylon,

Spending my blood to purchase thy renowne,

And this is the guerdon of my chiualrie,

Ended in this abusing of my wife?   885

Restore her me, or I will from thy Courts,

And make discourse of thy adulterous deeds.

Rasni.

Why take her Paphlagon, exclaime not man,

For I do prise mine honour more then loue.

Faire Aluida go with thy husband home.   890

Alui.

How dare I go, sham'd with so deep misdeed,

Reueuge will broile within my husbands brest,

And when he hath me in the Court at home,

Then Aluida shall feele reuenge for all.

Rasni.

What saist thou king of Paphlagon to this?   895

877: seate? / CEF; seate, ABD; seat? Dyce
880: wife? / BCEFDyce; -- AD
885: wife? / DEFDyce; --, ABC

Thou herest the doubt thy wife doth stand vpon,

If she hath done amisse it is my fault,

I prithie pardon and forget it all.

Paphla.

If that I meant not Rasni to forgiue,

And quite forget the follies that are past,   900

I would not vouch her presence in my Courts,

But she shall be my Queene, my loue, my life,

And Aluida vnto her Paphlagon

And lou'd, and more belou'd then before.

Rasni.

What saist thou Aluida to this?   905

Alui.

That will he sweare to my Lord the king,

And in a full carouse of Greekish wine,

Drinke downe the malice of his deepe reuenge,

I will go home and loue him new againe.

Rasni.

What answeres Paphlagon?   910

Paphla.

That what she hath requested I will do.

Alui.

Go damsell, fetch me that sweete wine

That stands within my Closet on the shelfe,

898: /it7 all. / EFG(Dyce)Dyce; all. ABCD
901: Court, / CG(3,4,Dyce); --; EF; Courts, ABD; courts; Dyce
912: damsell, fetch / Dyce; damsell fetch ABCDEF; damsell and fetch G(Dyce)
913: my / DEFG(5,Dyce)Dyce; thy ABF; the CG(3,4)

Powre it into a standing bowle of gold, /

But on thy life taste not before the king,   915   D4

Make hast, why is great Rasni melancholy thus?

If promise be not kept, hate all for me.

$\lceil$ Wine brought in by Female Attendant. $\rceil$

Here is the wine my Lord, first make him sweare.

Paphla.

By Niniuies great gods, and Niniuies great king,

My thoughts shall neuer be to wrong my wife,   920

And thereon heres a full carowse to her.

Alui.

And thereon Rasni heres a kisse for thee.

Now maist thou freely fold thine Aluida.

Paphla.

Oh I am dead, obstructions of my breath!

The poison is of wondrous sharpe effect,   925

Cursed be all adultrous queenes say I,

And cursing so poore Paphlagon doth die.

Alui.

Now haue I not salued the sorrowes of my Lord?

Haue I not rid a riuall of thy loues?

What saist thou Rasni to thy Paramour?   930

917-918: $\lceil$ Wine brought in by Female Attendant. $\rceil$ / E; omitted ABCDF;
    Wine brought in. Dyce
924: breath! / G(Dyce)Dyce; -- A; --, BCDG(2-5); --; E; --. F
929: a riuall / BEF; a rival Dyce; ariuall A; arriual G(3,5); ariual
    CG(4)
929: loues? / CF; --, ABDE; loves? Dyce

Rasni.

That for this deed ile decke my Aluida,

In Sendall and in costly Sussapine,

Bordred with Pearle and India Diamond,

Ile cause great Eol perfume all his windes,

With richest myrre and curious Ambergreece,   935

Come louely minion, paragon so faire,

Come follw me sweete goddesse of mine eye,

And taste the pleasures Rasni will prouide. Exeunt.

Oseas.

Where whordome raines, there murther followes fast,

As falling leaues before the winter blast.   940

A wicked life trained vp in endlesse crime,

Hath no regard vnto the latter time.

When Letchers shall be punisht for their lust,

When Princes plag'd because they are vniust.

Foresee in time the warning bell doth towle,   945

Subdue the flesh, by praier to saue the soule.

London behold the cause of others wracke,

And see the sword of iustice at thy backe.

Deferre not off to morrow is too late,

By night he comes perhaps to iudge thy state. /   950

⌐ III, i ⌐

       Enter Ionas Solus   D4v

Ionas.

From forth the depth of my imprisoned soule,

Steale you my sighes, testifie my paine,

Conuey on wings of mine immortall tone,

My zealous praiers, vnto the starrie throne: 955

Ah mercifull and iust thou dreadful God,

Where is thine arme to laie reuengefull stroakes

Vpon the heads of our rebellious race?

Loe Israell once that flourisht like the vine,

Is barraine laide, the beautifull encrease   960

Is wholly blent, and irreligious zeale

Incampeth there where vertue was inthroan'd

Ah-lasse the while, the widow wants reliefe,

The fatherlesse is wrongd by naked need,

Deuotion sleepes in sinders of Contempt,   965

Hypocrisie infects the holie Priest,

Aye me for this, woe me for these misdeeds,

Alone I walke to thinke vpon the world,

And sigh to see thy Prophets so contem'd:

Ah-lasse contem'd by cursed Israell.   970

Yet Ionas rest content, tis Israels sinne

That causeth this, then muse no more thereon,

But pray amends, and mend thy owne amisse.

  An Angell appeareth to Ionas.

Angel.

Amithais sonne, I charge thee muse no more,   975

(I am) hath power to pardon and correct,

To thee pertains to do the Lords command.

Go girt thy loines, and hast thee quickly hence,

To Niniuie, that mightie Citie wend,

And say this message from the Lord of hoasts,   980

Preach vnto them these tidings from thy God.

Behold thy wickednesse hath tempted me,

And pierced through the ninefold orbes of heauens,

Repent, or else thy iudgement is at hand. /

    This said, the Angell vanisheth.   985   El

Ionas.

Prostrate I lye before the Lord of hostes,

With humble eares intending his behest,

Oh honoured be Iehouahs great command,

Then Ionas must to Niniuie repaire,

Commanded as the Prophet of the Lord,   990

Great dangers on this iourny do awaight,

But dangers none where heauens direct the course,

What should I deeme? I see, yea sighing see,

How Israel sins, yet knowes the way of truth,

And thereby growes the by-word of the world,   995

How then should God in iudgement be so strict?

Gainst those who neuer heard or knew his power,

To threaten vtter ruin of them all:

981: these / BCDEFG(2-5,Dyce); thse A
986: Ionas./ BCDEFG(2-5)Dyce; -- A
993: deeme? / CEFDyce; --, ABD
994: sins, / G(Dyce); sinne, ABCD; sin(s), EF; sin Dyce

Should I report this iudgement of my God,

I should incite them more to follow sinne,   1000

And publish to the world my countries blame,

It may not be, my conscience tels me no.

Ah <u>Ionas</u> wilt thou proue rebellious then?

Consider ere thou fall what errour is.

My minde misgiues to Ioppa will I flee,   1005

And for a while to <u>Tharsus</u> shape my course,

Vntill the Lord vnfret **his** angry browes.

<u>Enter certaine Merchants of Tharsus, a Maister</u>

        <u>and some Sailers.</u>

<u>Maister.</u>

Come on braue merchants now the wind doth serue,   1010

And sweetly blowes a gale at West Southwest.

Our yardes a crosse, our anchors on the pike,

What shall we hence and take this merry gale?

<u>Mer.</u>

Sailers conuey our budgets strait aboord,

And we will recompence your paines at last,   1015

If once in safetie we may <u>Tharsus</u> see,

Master. weele feast these merry mates and thee.

<u>Master.</u>

Mean-while content your selues with silly cates,

1004: is. / EFDyce; --, ABCD
1010: on / BCDG(2-5)Dyce; --, EF; one A
1018: your selues / BCDEFG(2-5); yonr selues A; yourselves Dyce

Our beds are boordes, our feasts are full mirth, /

We vse no pompe, we are the Lords of see,   1020   El v

When Princes swet in care, we swincke of glee.

Orious shoulders and the pointers serue,

To be our loade-stars in the lingering night,

The beauties of Arcturus we behold,

And though the Sailer is no booke-man held,   1025

He knowes more Art then euer booke-men read.

Sailer.

By heauens well said, in honour of our trade,

Lets see the proudest scholler steer his course

Or shift his tides as silly sailers do,

Then wil we yeeld them praise, else neuer none.   1030

Mer.

Well spoken fellow in thine owne behalfe,

But let vs hence, wind tarries none you wot,

And tide and time let slip is hardly got.

Master.

March to the hauen merchants, I follow you.

Ionas.

Now doth occasion further my desires,   1035

I finde companions fit to aide my flight.

Staie sir I pray, and heare a word or two.

Master.

Say on good friend, but briefly if you please,

1028: steer / EFG(Dyce)Dyce; stir ABCD

My passengers by this time are aboord.

Ionas.

Whether pretend you to imbarke your selues?   1040

Master.

To Tharsus sir, and here in Ioppa hauen
Our ship is prest and readie to depart.

Ionas.

May I haue passage for my mony then?

Master.

What not for mony? pay ten siluerlings,
You are a welcome guest if so you please.   1045

Ionas.

Hold take thy hire, I follow thee my friend.

Maister.

Where is your budget let me beare it sir.

Ionas.

Go on in peace, who saile as I do now,
Put trust in him who succoureth euery want.

                                    Exeunt.   1050

Oseas.

When Prophets new inspirde, presume to force
And tie the power of heauen to their conceits,
When feare, promotion, pride, or simony,
Ambition, subtill craft, their thoughts disguise,
Woe to the flocke whereas the shepheards foule, /   1055

1048: go on in peace, / To one in peace, ABCDEFDyce See the Commentary.

For lo the Lord at vnawares shall plague   E2

The carelesse guide, because his flocks do stray.

The axe alreadie to the tree is set,

Beware to tempt the Lord ye men of art.

⌐ III, ii *⌐*

Enter Alcon, Thrasibulus, Samia,   1060

Clesiphon a lad.

Clesi.

Mother, some meat or else I die for want.

Samia.

Ah little boy how glad thy mother would

Supply thy wants but naked need denies:

Thy fathers slender portion in this world,   1065

By usury and false deceit is lost,

No charitie within this Citie bides:

All for themselues, and none to helpe the poore.

Clesi.

Father, shall Clesiphon haue no reliefe?

Alcon.

Faith my boy I must be flat with thee, we must   1070

feed vpon prouerbes now. As necessitie hath no law,

a churles feast is better then none at all, for other

remedies haue we none, except thy brother Radagon helpe

vs.

1069: Father, / BDEFDyce; -- AC
1070: Alcon. / BCDEFG(2-5); -- A; ALC. Dyce

<u>Samia.</u>

Is this thy slender case to helpe our childe?

Hath nature armde thee to no more remorse?   1075

Ah cruell man, vnkind, and pittilesse,

Come <u>Clesiphon</u> my boy, ile beg for thee.

<u>Clesi.</u>

Oh how my mothers mourning moueth me!

<u>Alcon.</u>

Nay you shall paie mee interest for getting the boye

(wife) before you carry him hence. Ah-lasse woman

what can <u>Alcon</u> do more? Ile plucke the belly out   1080

of my heart for thee sweete <u>Samia</u>, be not so waspish.

<u>Samia.</u>

Ah silly man I know thy want is great,

And foolish I do craue where nothing is.

Haste Alcon haste, make halfe vnto our sonne,   1085

Who since he is in fauour of the King,

May helpe this haplesse Gentleman and vs,

For to regaine our goods from tyrants hands.

<u>Thra.</u>

Haue patience <u>Samia</u>, waight your weale from heauen,

The Gods haue raisde your sonne I hope for this, /   1090

To succour innocents in their distresse.   E2v

1078: me! / <u>EFDyce</u>; --? <u>A</u>; --. <u>BD</u>; mee <u>C</u>
1084: foolishly I do / <u>BDG(2-5)</u>; foolish I do <u>CG(4)</u>; foolish I to <u>AEFDyce</u>
1087: vs, / <u>EDyce</u>; --. <u>ABD</u>; -- <u>CFG(3,4)</u>
1090: The / <u>BEFG(2)Dyce</u>; Tho <u>ACD</u>

Enters Radagon, Solus.

Lo where he comes from the imperiall Court,

Go let vs prostrate vs before his feete.

Alcon.

Nay by my troth, ile neuer aske my sonne blessing,

che trow, cha taught him his lesson to know his   1095

father, what sonne Radagon, yfaith boy how doest

thee?

Rada.

Villaine disturbe me not, I cannot stay.

Alcon.

Tut sonne ile helpe you of that disease quickly, for

I can hold thee, aske thy mother knaue what cunning I

haue to ease a woman when a qualme of kindnesse come   1100

to neare her stomache? Let me but claspe mine armes

about her bodie and saie my praiers in her bosome, and

she shall be healed presently.

Rada.

Traitor vnto my Princely Maiestie,

How dar'st thou laie thy hands vpon a King?   1105

Samia.

No Traitor Radagon, but true is he,

What hath promotion bleared thus thine eye,

To scorne thy father when he visits thee?

Ah-lasse my sonne behold with ruthfull eyes,

Thy parents robd of all their worldly weale,

By subtle meanes of Vsurie and guile,

The Iudges eares are deaffe and shut vp close,

All mercie sleepes, then be thou in these plundges

A patron to thy mother in her paines,

Behold thy brother almost dead for foode,   1115

Oh succour vs, that first did succour thee.

Rada.

What succour me? false callet hence auant?

Old dotard pack, moue not my patience,

I know you not, Kings neuer looke so low.

Samia.

You know vs not. Oh Radagon you know,   1120

That knowing vs, you know your parents then,

Thou knowst this wombe first brought thee forth to light,

I know these paps did foster thee my sonne.

Alcon.

And I know he hath had many a peece of bread and

cheese at my hands, as proud as he is, that know I.   1125

Thracib.

I waight no hope of succours in this place, /

Where children hold their fathers in disgrace. =   E3

Rada.

Dare you enforce the furrowes of reuenge,

Within the browes of royall Radagon?

Villaine auant, hence beggers with your brats,   1130

1117: me? / CD; --. AE; --! FDyce

Marshall why whip you not these rogues away?

That thus disturbe our royall Maiestie.

Clesiphon. Mother I see it is a wondrous thing,

From base estate for to become a King:

For why meethinke my brother in these fits,   1135

Hath got a kingdome, and hath lost his wits.

Rada.

Yet more contempt before my royaltie?

Slaues fetch out tortures worse then Titius plagues,

And teare their toongs from their blasphemous heads.

Thrasi.

Ile get me gone, though woe begon with griefe,   1140

No hope remaines, come Alcon let vs wend.

Rada.

Twere best you did, for feare you catch your bane.

Samia.

Nay traitor, I wil haunt thee to the death,

Vngratious sonne, vntoward and peruerse,

Ile fill the heauens with echoes of thy pride,   1145

And ring in euery eare thy small regard,

That does despise thy parents in their wants,

And breathing forth my soule before thy feete,

My curses still shall haunt thy hatefull head,

And being dead, my ghost shall thee pursue.   1150

Enter Rasni, King of Assiria, attended on by his

1151: Rasni, / E; -- ABCDF; RASNI, Dyce

sooth-sayers and Kings.

Rasni.

How now? what meane these outcries in our Court?

Where nought should sound but harmonies of heauen,

What maketh Radagon so passionate?   1155

Samia.

Iustice O King, iustice against my sonne.

Rasni. Thy sonne: what sonne?

Samia.

This cursed Radagon.

Rada.

Dread Monarch, this is but a lunacie,

Which griefe and want hath brought the woman to.   1160

What doth this passion hold you euerie Moone? /

Samia.

Oh polliticke in sinne and wickednesse,   E3v

Too impudent for to delude thy Prince.

Oh Rasni this same wombe first brought him forth.

This is his father, worne with care and age,   1165

This is his brother, poore vnhappie lad,

And I his mother, though contemn'd by him,

With tedious toyle we got our litle good,

And brought him vp to schoole with mickle charge:

Lord how we ioy'd to see his towardnesse,   1170

1153: now? / C; --. ABDEF; --, Dyce
1160: to. / FDyce; --, ABCD; --. -E

And to our selues we oft in silence said,

This youth when we are old may succour vs.

But now preferd and lifted vp by thee,

We quite destroyd by cursed vsurie,

He scornth me, his father, and this childe.   1175

Clesi.

He plaies the Serpent right, describ'd in Aesopes tale,

That sought the Fosters death that lately gaue him life.

Alcon.

Nay and please your Maiesti-ship, for proofe he was my

childe, search the parish booke, the Clarke wil sweare

it, his godfathers and godmothers can witnesse it, it

cost me fortie pence in ale and cakes on the wiues at   1180

his christning. Hence proud King, thou shalt neuer

more haue my blessing. He takes him apart.

Rasni.

Say sooth in secret Radagon,

Is this thy father?   1185

Rada.

Mightie king he is,

I blashing, tell it to your Maiestie.

Rasni.

Why dost thou then contemne him and his friends?

Rada.

Because he is a base and abiect swaine,

1188: Why / BCDEFG(2)Dyce; Thy A

My mother and her brat both beggarly,   1190

Vnmeete to be allied vnto a King.

Should I that looke on Rasnies countenance,

And march amidst his royall equipage,

Embase my selfe to speake to such as they?

Twere impious so to impaire the loue   1195

That mightie Rasni beares to Radagon.

I would your grace would quit them from your sight /

That dare presume to looke on Ioues compare.   E4

Rasni.

I like thy pride, I praise thy pollicie,

Such should they be that wait vpon my Court.   1200

Let me alone to answere Radagon.

Villaines, seditious traitors as you be,

That scandalize the honour of a King,

Depart my Court you stales of impudence,

Vnlesse you would be parted from your limmes,   1205

So base for to intitle father-hood,

To Rasnies friend, to Rasnies fauourite?

Rada.

Hence begging scold, hence caitiue clogd with yeares,

Oh paine of death reuisit not the Court.

Was I conceiu'd by such a scruie trull,   1210

Or brought to light by such a lump of dirt?

1192: Rasnies / G(4); Rasnes ABCD; Rasnis EF; Rasni's Dyce
1207: Rasnies / Rasnes ABCD; Rasnis EF; Rasni's Dyce

Go Lassell trot it to the cart and spade,

Thou art vnmeete to looke vpon a King,

Much lesse to be the father of a King.

Alcon.

You may see wife what a goodly peece of worke you   1215

haue made, haue I tought you Arsmetry, as additiori

multiplicarum, the rule of three, and all for

the begetting of a boy, and to be banished for my labour.

O pittifull hearing. Come Clesiphon follow me.

Clesi.

Brother beware, I oft haue heard it told,

That sonnes who do their fathers scorne, shall beg when   1220

they be old.   Exit. Alcon, Clesiphon.

Radagon.

Hence bastard boy for feare you taste the whip.

Samia.

Oh all you heauens, and you eternall powers,

That sway the sword of iustice in your hands,   1225

(If mothers curses for her sonnes contempt,

May fill the ballance of your furie full)

Powre doune the tempest of your direfull plagues,

Vpon the head of cursed Radagon.

Vpon this praier she departeth, and a flame of fire   1230

appeareth from beneath, and Radagon is swallowed.

1222: Exit / BCDG(2-5); Exet A; Exeunt EFDyce

So you are iust, now triumph Samia. Exit Samia. /

Rasni.

What exorcising charme, or hatefull hag,   E4v

Hath rauished the pride of my delight?

What tortuous planets, or maleuolent   1235

Conspiring power, repining destinie

Hath made the concaue of the earth vnclose,

And shut in ruptures louely Radagon?

If I be Lord-commander of the cloudes,

King of the earth, and soueraign of the sears,   1240

What daring Saturne from his fierie denne,

Doth dart these furious flames amidst my Court?

I am not chiefe, there is more great than I,

What greater then Th'Assirian Satrapos?

I may not be, and yet I feare there is,   1245

That hath bereft me of my Radagon.

Soothsaier.

Monarch and Potentate of all our Prouinces,

Muse not so much vpon this accident,

Which is indeed nothing miraculous,

The hill of Sicely, dread Soueraigne,   1250

Sometime on sodaine doth euacuate,

Whole flakes of fire, and spues out from below

1232: Exit / CDEFG(3,5); Exet A; Exi. BG(2); ⌐ Exit. Dyce
1244: Th' Assirian / E; the Assyrian Dyce; Th'assirian ABCDF
1249: miraculous. / EFDyce; --, ABCD

The smoakie brands that <u>Vulcans</u> belowes driue,

Whether by windes inclosed in the earth,

Or fracture of the earth by riuers force, 1255

Such chances as was this, are often seene,

Whole Citie suncke, whole Countries drowned quite.

Then muse not at the losse of <u>Radagon</u>,

But frolicke with the dalliance of your loue.

Let cloathes of purple set with studdes of gold, 1260

Embellished with all the pride of earth,

Be spred for <u>Aluida</u> to sit vpon.

Then thou like <u>Mars</u> courting the queene of loue,

Maist driue away this melancholy fit.

<u>Rasni</u>.

The proofe is good and philosophicall, 1265

And more, thy counsaile plausible and sweete.

Come Lords, though <u>Rasni</u> wants his <u>Radagon</u>,

Earth will repaie him many <u>Radagons</u>, /

And <u>Aluida</u> with pleasant lookes reuiue, F1

The heart that droupes for want of <u>Radagon</u>. 1270

<u>Oseas</u>.

When <u>disobedience</u> <u>raigneth</u> <u>in</u> <u>the</u> <u>childe</u>,

And <u>Princes</u> <u>eares</u> <u>by</u> <u>flattery</u> <u>be</u> <u>beguilde</u>;

1253: Vulcans / G(4)EFDyce; Vuluens ABCD
1257: quite. / FDyce; --, ABCD; --: E
1258: Radagon,/ CEFG(3,4)Dyce; --. ABD
1273: beguilde; / EFDyce; --. ABD; --: CG(3,4)

When lawes do passe by fauour, not by truth;

When falshood swarmeth both in old and youth;   1275

When gold is made a god to wrong the poore,

And charitie exilde from rich mens doore;

When men by wit do labour to disproue,

The plagues for sinne, sent downe by God aboue;

When great mens eares are stopt to good aduice,   1280

And apt to heare those tales that feed their vice;

Woe to the land, for from the East shall rise,

A lambe of peace, the scourge of Vanities,

The iudge of truth, the patron of the iust,

Who soone will laie presumption in the dust,   1285

And guiue the humble poore their hearts desire,

And doome the worldlings to eternall fire.

Repent all you that heare, for feare of plagues.

O' London, this and more doth swarme in thee;

Repent, repent, for why the Lord doth see.   1290

With trembling pray, and mend what is amisse;

The swoord of iustice drawne alreadie is.

1274: truth; / FDyce; --, ABCDE
1275: youth; / EFDyce; --. ABD; --, CDG(3,4)
1277: doore; / EFDyce; doore, AB; --, CDG(3-5)
1279: aboue; / EFDyce; aboue. ABD; --: CG(3,4)
1280: When / EG(Dyce); Where ABCDF
1280: stopt / BCDEFG(2-5)Dyce; stop A
1281: vice; / EFDyce; vice. ABD; --: C
1283: vanities, / EDyce; --. ABCD; --; F
1285: dust, / CEFG(3,4)Dyce; dust. ABL
1288: plagues. / CEFDyce; --, ABD
1289: thee; / EDyce; --, ABCD; --! F
1291: amisse; / FDyce; --, ABCDE

/¯ III, iii ¯/

Enter /¯ Adam ¯/ the Clowne and the Smiths wife.

Clowne.

Why but heare you mistresse, you know a womans eies
are like a paire of pattens fit to saue shooleather in
sommer, and to keepe away the cold in winter, so you   1295
make like your husband with the one eye, because you
are married, and me with the other, because I am your
man. Alasse, alasse, think mistresse what a thing loue
is, why it is like to an ostry fagot, that once set on   1300
fire, is as hardly quenched, as the bird Crocodill driuen
out of her neast.

Wife.

Why Adam cannot a woman winke but she must sleep? and
can she not loue but she must crie it out at the Crosse?

know /

Adam, I loue thee as my selfe, now that we are together   Flv

in secret.   1305

Clown.

Mistris. These words of yours are like a fox taile
placed in a gentlewomans Fanne, which as it is light,

1293: /¯ Adam, ¯/ the Clowne / EDyce; the Clowne ABCDF; Adam E
       See the Commentary.
1302: Why / BCDG(2-5); --, EFDyce; Thy A
1302: Sleep? / DE; --, ABCEDyce
1303: Crosse? /¯CEF; --, ABD; cross? Dyce
1306: like a fox tale / like to a Fox taile AC; like a Fox taile BEF;
       like a Foxe-tayle, D; like a fox-tail Dyce

so it giueth life. Oh these words are as sweete as a

lilly, wherupon offering a borachio of kisses to

vnseemly personage, I entertaine you vpon further

acquaintance.   1310

Wife.

Alasse my husband comes.

Clowne.

Strike vp the drum, and say no words but mum.

                    ⌐ Enter Smith. ⌐

Smith.

Sirrha you, and you huswife, well taken togither, I

haue long suspected you, and now I am glad I haue found   1315

you togither.

Clowne.

Truly sir, and I am glad that I may do you any way

pleasure, either in helping you or my mistresse.

Smith.

Boy here, and knaue you shall know it straight, I wil

haue you both before the Magistrate, and there haue you

surely punished.   1320

Clowne.

Why then maister you are iealous?

Smith.

Iealous knaue, how can I be but iealous, to see you euer

1312-1313: ⌐ Enter Smith. ⌐ / F; omitted ABCD; ⌐ Enter the Smith. ⌐
     E; Enter the Smith Dyce

so familiar togither? Thou art not only content to

drinke away my goods, but to abuse my wife.

Clowne.

Two good qualities, drunkennesse and lechery, but maister   1325

are you iealous?

Smith.

I haue and thou shalt know it ere I passe, for I will

beswindge thee while this roape will hold,

Wife.

My good husband abuse him not, for he neuer proffered

you any wrong.   1330

Smith.

Nay whore, thy part shall not be behinde.

Clowne.

Why suppose maister I haue offended you, is it lawfull

for the maister to beate the seruant for all offences?

Smith.

I marry is it knaue.

Clowne.

Then maister wil I proue by logicke, that seeing all   1335

sinnes are to receiue correction, the maister is to be

corrected of the man, and sir I pray you, what greater

sinne is, then iealousie? tis like a mad dog that for

anger bites himselfe. Therefore that I may doe my dutie

1330: wrong./ CDEFDyce; --, AB

to you good maister, and to make a white /

sonne of you, I will so beswinge iealousie out of you,   F2

as you shall loue me the better while you liue.   1340

Smith.

What beate thy maister knaue?

Clowne.

What beat thy man knaue? and I maister, and double beate

you, because you are a man of credite,

and therefore haue at you the fairest for fortie pence.   1345

Smith.   ⌐ Beats the Smith. ⌐

Alasse wife,helpe, helpe, my man kils me.

Wife.

Nay, euen as you haue baked so brue, iealousie must be

driuen out by extremities.

Clowne.

And that will I do, mistresse.

Smith.

Hold thy hand Adam, and not only I forgiue and forget   1350

all, but I will giue thee a good Farme to liue on.

Clowne.

Begone Peasant, out of the compasse of my further

wrath, for I am a corrector of vice, and at night I

wil bring home my mistresse.

Smith.

1345-46: ⌐ Beats the Smith. ⌐ / EF; omitted ABCDDyce

Euen when you please good Adam.   1355

Clowne.

When I please, marke the words, tis a lease paroll, to

haue and to hold, thou shalt be mine for euer, and so

lets go to the Ale-house.

                                              Exeunt.
Oseas.

Where seuants against maisters do rebell,   1360

The common-weale may be accounted hell.

For if the feete the head shall hold in scorne,

The cities state will fall and be forlorne.

This error London, waiteth on thy state,

Seruants amend, and maisters leaue to hate.   1365

Let loue abound, and vertue raigne in all,

So God will hold his hand that threateneth thrall.

⎾ IV, i ⏌

Enter the Merchants of Tharsus, the Master of the ship,

some Sailers, wet from sea, with them the Gouernour   1370

                    of Ioppa.

Gouer.Iop.

What strange encounters met you on the sea?

That thus your Barke is battered by the flouds,

And you returne thus seawrackt as I see. /

Mer.

Most mightie gouernor the chance is strange,   F2v

_____

1360: against / FG(Dyce)Dyce; (a)gainst E; gainst ABCD

The tidings full of wonder and amaze,   1375

Which better then we, our Master can report.

Gouer.

Master discourse vs all the accident.

Master.

The faire Triones with their glimmering light

Smil'd at the foote of cleare Boote's wain,

And in the north distinguishing the houres,   1380

The Load-starre of our course dispearst his cleare,

When to the seas with blithfull westerne blasts,

We saild amaine, and let the bowling flie:

Scarre had we gone ten leagues from sight of land,

But lo and hoast of blacke and sable cloudes,   1385

Gan to eclips Lucinas siluer face,

And with a hurling noyse from foorth the South,

A gust of winde did reare the billowes vp,

Then scantled we our sailes with speedie hands,

And tooke our drablers from our bonnets straight,   1390

And seuered our bonnets from the courses,

Our topsailes vp, we trusse our spritsailes in,

But vainly striue they that resist the heauens.

For loe the waues incence them more and more,

Mounting with hideous roarings from the depth,   1395

Our Barke is battered by incountring stormes,

1379: Boote's wain,/ EFG(Dyce)Dyce; Rootes a raine, ABCD
1380: north / EFG(Dyce)Dyce; wrath ABCD

And welny stemd by breaking of the flouds,

The steersman pale, and carefull holds his helme,

Wherein the trust of life and safetie laie,

Till all at once (a mortall tale to tell)   1400

Our sailes were split by Bisas bitter blast,

Our rudder broke and we bereft of hope.

There might you see with pale and gastly lookes,

The dead in thought, and dolefull merchants lift,

Their eyes and hands vnto their Countries Gods,   1405

The goods we crast in bowels of the sea,

A sacrifice to swage proud Neptunes ire,

Onely alone a man of Israell,

A passenger, did vnder hatches lie, /

And slept secure, when we for succour praide: 1410   F3

Him I awooke, and said why slumberest thou?

Arise and pray, and call vpon thy God,

He will perhaps in pitie looke on vs.

Then cast we lots to know by whose amisse

Our mischiefe came, according to the guise,   1415

And loe the lot did vnto Ionas fall,

The Israelite of whom I told you last,

Then questioned we his country and his name,

Who answered vs, I am an Hebrue borne,

1404: lift / EFG(Dyce)Dyce; lifts, ABCD; lifts CG(3)
1415: came, / E; come, ABCDFG(3,4)
1418: questioned / questiond CG(3,4); question ABDEF

Who feare the Lord of heauen, who made the sea,   1420

And fled from him for which we all are plagu'd,

Go to asswage the furie of my God,

Take me and cast my carkasse in the sea,

Then shall this stormy winde and billow cease.

The heauens they know, the Hebrues God can tell,   1425

How loth we were to execute his will:

But when no Oares nor labour might suffice,

We heaued the haplesse <u>Ionas</u> ouer-boord.

So ceast the storme, and calmed all the sea,

And we by strength of oares recouered shoare.   1430

<u>Gouer</u>.

A wonderous chance of mighty consequence.

<u>Mer</u>.

Ah honored be the God that wrought the fame,

For we haue vowd, that saw his wonderous workes,

To cast away prophaned Paganisme,

And count the Hebrues God the onely God.   1435

To him this offering of the purest gold,

This mirrhe and Cascia freely I do yeeld.

<u>Master</u>.

And on his altars perfume these Turkie clothes,

This gossampine and gold ile sacrifice.

<u>Sailer</u>.

To him my heart and thoughts I will addict,   1440

Then suffer vs most mightie Gouernour,

Within your Temples to do sacrifice.

Gouer.

You men of Tharsus follow me,

Who sacrifice vnto the God of heauen,

And welcome friends to Ioppais Gouernor.

Exeunt a sacrifice. /

1445

Oseas.

If warned once, the Ethnicks thus repent,

F3v

And at the first their errour do lament:

What senslesse beasts deuoured in their sinne,

Are they whom long perswations cannot winne.

Beware ye westerne Cities where the word

1450

Is daily preached both at church and boord:

Where maiestie the Gospell doth maintaine,

Where Preachers for your good, themselues do paine,

To dally long, and still protract the time,

The Lord is iust, and you but dust and slime:

1455

Presume not far, delaie not to amend,

Who suffereth long, will punish in the end.

Cast thy account o London in this case,

Then iudge what cause thou hast, to call for grace.

⎣IV, ii⎦

Ionas the Prophet ⎣is⎦ cast out of the Whales

1460

belly vpon the Stage.

1460: ⎣ is ⎦ / Dyce; omitted ABCDEF

<u>Ionas</u>.

Lord of the light, thou maker of the world,
Behold thy hands of mercy reare me vp,
Loe from the hidious bowels of this fish,
Thou hast returnd me to the wished aire,   1465
Loe here apparent witnesse of thy power,
The proud Leuiathan that scoures the seas,
And from his nosthrils showres out stormy flouds,
Whose backe resists the tempest of the winde,
Whose presence makes the scaly troopes to shake,   1470
With humble stresse of his broad opened chappes,
Hath lent me harbour in the raging flouds.
Thus though my sin hath drawne me down to death,
Thy mercy hath restored me to life.
Bow ye my knees, and you my bashfull eyes,   1475
Weepe so for griefe, as you to water would:
In trouble Lord I called vnto thee,
Out of the belly of the deepest hell,
I cride, and thou didst to heare my voice O God: /
Tis thou hadst cast me downe the deepe,   1480   F4
The seas and flouds did compasse me about,
I thought I had bene cast from out thy sight,
The weeds were wrapt about my wretched head,
I went vnto the bottome of the hilles,
But thou O Lord my God hast brought me vp.   1485

1463: reare / rear <u>G(Dyce)Dyce</u>; rears <u>ACDEF</u>; raise <u>B</u>

On thee I thought when as my soule did faint,

My praiers did prease before thy mercy seate,

Then will I paie my vowes vnto the Lord,

For why saluation cometh from his throane.   1490

       The Angell appeareth.

Angell.

Ionas arise, get thee to Niniuie,

And preach to them the preachings that I had:

Haste thee to see the will of heauen perform'd.

       Depart Angell.

Ionas.

Iehouah I am prest to do thy will.   1495

What coast is this, and where am I arriu'd?

Behold sweete Licas streaming in his boundes,

Bearing the walles of haughtie Niniuie,

Whereas three hundred towres do tempt the heauen.

Faire are thy walles pride of Assiria,   1500

But lo thy sinnes haue pierced through the cloudes.

Here will I enter boldly, since I know

By God commands, whose power no power resists.

       Exit.

Oseas.

You Prophets learne by Ionas how to liue,   1505

Repent your sinnes, whilst he doth warning giue,

1495: prest / DEFG(5,Dyce); priest ABC
1499: towres / DFG(5); towns AB; Towns C; towers EDyce
1504: Exit./ BEFG(2); Exet. ACD; / Exit. Dyce

Who knowes his maisters will and doth it not,

Shall suffer many stripes full well I wot.

$\int$ IV, iii $\rfloor$

Enter Aluida in rich attire, with the King of

                   Cilicia, her Ladies.   1510

Aluida.

Ladies go sit you downe amidst this bowre,

And let the Eunuckes plaie you all a sleepe:

Put garlands made of Roses on your heads, /

And plaie the wantons whilst I take a while.   F4v

Lady.

Thou beautifull of all the world, we will.   1515

              Enter the bowers.

Aluid.

King of Cilicia, kind and curtious,

Like to thy selfe, because a lonely King,

Come laie thee down vpon thy mistresse knee,   1520

And I will sing and talke of loue to thee.

King Cili.

Most gratious Paragon of excellence,

It fits not such an abiect Prince as I,

To tale with Rasnies Paramour and loue.

Al.

To talke sweet friend?who wold not talke with thee?

1523: Rasnies / Rasnes ABCD; Rasnis EF; Rasni's Dyce

Oh be not coy, art thou not only faire?   1525

Come twine thine armes about this snow white neck,

A loue-nest for the great Assirian King,

Blushing I tell thee, faire Cilician Prince,

None but thy selfe can merit such a grace.

K. Ci.

Madam I hope you mean not for to mock me: 1530

Al.

No king, faire king, my meaning is to yoke thee.

Heare me but sing of loue, then by my sighes,

My teares, my glauncing lookes, my changed cheare,

Thou shalt perceiue how I do hold thee deare.

K. Ci.

Sing Madam if you please, but loue in iest.   1535

Aluid.

Nay, I will loue, and sigh at euery rest.

                              Song.

    Beautie alasse where wast thou borne?

    Thus to hold thy selfe in scorne:

    When as Beautie kist to wooe thee,   1540

    Thou by Beautie doest vndo mee.

        Heigho, despise me not.

    I amd thou in sooth are one,

    Fairer thou, I fairer none:

_____

1528: thee, faire / EFDyce; thee faire, A; thee faire BCDG(2-5)
1535: iest. / CEFG(3,4)Dyce; --, ABD

Wanton thou, and wilt thou wanton   1545

Yeeld a cruell heart to plant on?

Do me right, and do me reason,

Crueltie is cursed treason.

    Heigho I loue, heigho I loue,

    Heigho, and yet he eies me not. /   1550

King.

Madam your song is passing passionate.   G1

Alui.

And wilt thou not then pitie my estate?

King.

Aske loue of them who pitie may impart.

Alui.

I aske of thee sweet, thou hast stole my hart.

King.

Your loue is fixed on a greater King.   1555

Alui.

Tut womens loue, it is a fickle thing.

I loue my Rasni for my dignitie.

I loue Cilician King for his sweete eye.

I loue my Rasni since he rules the world.

But more I loue this kingly litle world. Embrace him.   1560

How sweete he lookes? Oh were I Cinthias Pheere,

And thou Endimion, I should hold thee deere:

Thus should mine armes be spred about thy necke.

                Embrace his necke.

Thus would I kisse my loue at euery becke.   1565

Kisse.

Thus would I sigh to see thee sweetly sleepe:

And if thou wakest not soone, thus would I weepe.

And thus, and thus, and thus: thus much I loue thee.

Kisse him.   1570

King.

For all these vowes, beshrow me if I proue you:

My faith vnto my king shall not be falc'd.

Alui.

Good Lord how men are coy when they are crau'd?

King.

Madam behold our King approacheth nie.

Alui.

Thou art Endimion, then no more, heigho for him I die.   1575

Faints. Points at the king of Cilicia.

Enter Rasni, with his Kings and Lords.

/ Rasni. 7

What ailes the Center of my happinesse,

Wherron depends the heauen of my delight?

Thine eyes the motors to command my world,   1580

Thy hands the axier to maintaine my world.

Thy smiles, the prime and spring-tide of my world.

Thy frownes, the winter to afflict the world.

1576: Points / CDG(3,4); Point ABEF
1578: / Rasni. 7 / EFDyce; omitted ABCD; RASNI. Dyce

Thou Queene of me, I King of all the world.

Alui.

Ah feeble eyes lift vp and looke on him,   1585

   ⌐ She riseth as out of a traunce.

Is Rasni here? then droupe no more poore hart, /

Oh how I fainted when I wanted thee?   Glv

               ⌐ Embrace him.

How faine am I, now I may looke on thee?

How glorious is my Rasni? how diuine?   1590

Eunuckes play himmes, to praise his deitie:

He is my Ioue, and I his Iuno am.

Rasni.

Sun-bright, as is the eye of sommers day,

When as he sutes Spenori all in gold,

To wooe his Leda in a swanlike shape.   1595

Seemely as Galatea for thy white:

Rose-coloured, lilly, louely, wanton, kinde,

Be thou the laborinth to tangle loue,

Whilst I command the crowne from Venus crest,

And pull Orion's girdle from his loined,   1600

Enchast with Carbunckles and Diamonds,

To beautifie faire Aluida my loue.

Play Eunuckes, sing in honour of her name,

Yet looke not slaues vpon her woing eyne,

1596: Galatea / EFG(Dyce); Galbocia ABCDDyce
1599: crest, / CEFG(4)Dyce; --; ABD
1600: Orion's / EDyce; Orions F; Onoris ABCD

For she is faire <u>Lucina</u> to your king,   1605

But fierce <u>Medusa</u> to your baser eie.

<u>Alui.</u>

What if I slept, where should my pillow be?

<u>Rasni.</u>

Within my boxome Nimph, not on my knee.

Sleepe like the smiling puritie of heauen,

When mildest wind is loath to blend the peace,   1610

Meane-while thy balme shall from thy breath arise,

And while these closures of they lampes be shut,

My soule may haue his peace from fancies <u>warre.</u>

This is my <u>Morn</u>, and I her <u>Cephalus.</u>

Wake not too soone sweete Nimph, my loue is wonne: 1615

<u>Caitiffs</u> why staie your straines, why tempt you me?

<u>Enter</u> the <u>Priests</u> <u>of</u> the <u>sunne</u>, <u>with</u> the <u>miters</u> <u>on</u>

their <u>heads</u>, <u>carrying</u> <u>fire</u> <u>in</u> <u>their</u> <u>hands</u> $\sqrt{}$ <u>and</u> <u>Sages</u>. $\underline{7}$

<u>Priest.</u>

All haile vnto <u>Th'Assirian</u> deitie.

<u>Ras.</u>

Priests why presume you to disturbe my peace?   1620

<u>Priest.</u>

<u>Rasni</u>, the destinies disturbe thy peace. /

1614: <u>Morn,</u> / E<u>Dyce</u>; Morne, F; Morane, ABCD
1616: <u>Caitiffs</u> $\overline{/}$ EG(<u>Dyce</u>); Catiues F; <u>Catnies</u> A; Catnies, BCDG(2-5)
1617: <u>Priests</u> / CFG(3,4,<u>Dyce</u>); <u>Priest</u> ABD; Priest(s) <u>E</u>
1618: $\sqrt{}$ <u>and Sages</u>. $\overline{7}$ / Lyce; omitted ABCDEF
1619: <u>Th'Assirian</u> / <u>E</u>; th'Assyrian <u>Dyce</u>; Th'assirian ABCDF

Behold admidst the adyts of our Gods,   G2

Our mightie Gods the patrons of our warre,

The ghosts of dead men howling walke about,

Crying Vae, Vae, wo to this Citie woe.   1625

The statues of our Gods are throwne downe,

And streames of blood our altars do distaine.

Aluida.

Ah-lasse my Lord what tidings do I hear?

Shall I be slaine?

         She starteth.   1630

Rasni.

Who tempteth Aluida?

Go breake me vp the brazen doores of dreames,

And binde me cursed Morpheus in a chaine,

And fetter all the fancies of the night,

Because they do disturbe my Aluida.   1635

A hand from out a cloud, threatneth a burning sword.

K. Cili.

Behold dread Prince, a burning sword from heauen.

Which by a threatning arm is brandished.

Rasni.

What am I threatned then amidst my throane?

Sages? you Magi? speake: what meaneth this?   1640

1622: adyts / EDyce; addittes AF
1623: warre, / DEFG(5); war, Dyce; warre. AB; warre: CG(3)
1624: ghosts/ DFG(5)Dyce; ghost(s) E; ghost ABC
1625: Vae, / Dyce; Ue, D; Ve, ABCEF
1638: arme is / DEF; arm is BCDyce; armis A

Sages.

These are but clammy exhalations,

Or retro grade, coniunctions of the starres,

Or oppositions of the greater lights.

Or radiations finding matter fit,

That in the starrie Spheare kindled be,   1645

Matters betokening dangers to thy foes,

But peace and honour to my Lord the King.

Rasni.

Then frolicke Viceroeis, Kings and potentates,

Driue all vaine fancies from your feeble mindes.

Priests go and pray, whilst I prepare my feast,   1650

Where Aluida and I, in pearle and gold,

Will quaffe vnto our Nobles, richest wine,

In spight of fortune, state, or destinie.

       Exeunt.

Oseas.

Woe to the traines of womens foolish lust,   1655

In wedlocke rights that yeeld but litle trust. /

That vow to one, yet common be to all,   G2v

Take warning wantons, pride will haue a fall.

Woe to the land where warnings profit nought,

Wo say that nature, Gods decrees hath wrought.   1660

Who build one fate, and leaue the corner stone,

1644: radiations / EFDyce; radiatrous ABCD

The God of Gods, sweete Christ the onely one.

If such escapes of London raigne in thee:

Repent, for why each sin shall punisht bee.

Repent, amend, repent, the houre is nie. 1665

Defer not time, who knowes when he shall die?

_⎡ IV, iv ⎤_

Enters one clad in diuels attire alone.

⎡ Devill. ⎤

Longer liues a merry man then a sad, and because I

meane to make my selfe pleasant this night, I haue

put myselfe into this attire, to make a Clowne afraid

that passeth this way: for of late there haue appeared 1670

many strange apparitions, to the great fear and terror

of the Citizens. Oh here my yoong maister comes.

Enters Adam and _⎡ the Smith's wife, ⎤_ his mistresse.

Adam.

Feare not mistresse, ile bring you safe home, if my

maister frowne, then will I strampe and stare, and if

all be not well then, why then to morrow morene put 1675

out mine eyes cleane with fortie pound.

Wife.

Oh but Adam, I am afraid to walke so late because of

the spirits that appeare in the Citie.

1667: _⎡ Devill. ⎤_ / F; DEV. Dyce; omitted ABCDE

1673: _⎡ the Smith's wife, ⎤_ his mistresse / _⎡ the SMITH'S WIFE ⎤_ his
mistress. Dyce; the Smith's wife, F; his mistresse. ABCE; his
Mistresse. D

Adam.

What are you afraid of spirits, armed as I am, with   1680

Ale, and Nutmegs, turne me loose to all the diuels in

hell.

Wife.

Alasse Adam, Adam, the diuell, the diuell.

Adam.

The diuell mistresse, flie you for safeguard, let me

alone, the diuell and I will deale well inough, if he

haue any honestie at all in him, Ile either win him

with a smooth tale, or else with a toste and a cup of   1685

Ale.

                    The Diuell sings here.

Diuell.

Oh, oh, oh, oh, faine would I bee,

If that my kingdome fulfilled I might see.

Oh, oh, oh, oh.   1690

Adam.

Surely this is a merry diuell, and I beleeue he is /

one of Lucifers Minstrels, hath a sweete voice,   G3

how surely, surely, he may sing to a paire of Tongs

and a Bag-pipe.

Diuell.

Oh thou art he that I seeke for.

1691, 1695, 1698, 1703, and 1706: Adam. / ElDyce; Clowne. ABC1F

Adam.

Spiritus santus, away from me satan, I haue nothing   1695
to do with thee.

Diuell.

Ch villaine thou art mine.

Adam.

Nominus patrus, I blesse me from thee, and I coniure
thee to tell me who thou art?

Diuell.

I am the spirit of the dead man that was slaine in thy   1700
company when we were drunke togither at the Ale.

Adam.

By my troth sir, I cry you mercy, your face is so
changed, that I had quite forgotten you, well maister
diuell we haue tost ouer many a pot of Ale togither.

Diuell.

And therefore must thou go with me to hell.   1705

Adam.

I haue a pollicie to shift him, for I know he comes out
of a hote place, and I know my selfe, the Smith and the
diuel hath a drie tooth in his head, therefore will I
leaue him a sleepe and runne my way.

Diuell.

Come art thou readie.   1710

Adam.

1711, 1718, 1722, 1729, and 1733: Adam./ EDyce ; Clowne. ABCDF

Faith sir my old friend, and now goodman diuell, you

know, you and I haue bene tossing many a good cup of

Ale, your nose is growne verie rich, what say you, will

you take a pot of Ale now at my hands, hell is like a

Smiths forge full of water, and yet euer a thrust.   1715

Diuell.

No Ale villaine, spirits cannot drinke, come get vp

on my backe, that I may carrie thee.

Adam.

You know I am a Smith sir, let me looke whether you be

well shod or no, for if you want a shoe a remoue, or

the clinching of a naile, I am at your command.   1720

Diuell.

Thou hast neuer a shoe fit for me.

Adam.

Why sir, we shooe horned beasts as well as you. Oh

good Lord let me sit downe and laugh, hath neuer a

clouen foote, a diuell quoth he, ile vse spritus santus

nor nominus patrus no more to him, I warrant you Ile do

more good vpon him with my cudgell, now will I sit me   1725

downe and become Iustice of peace to the diuell. /

Diuell.

Come art thou readie?   83v

Adam.

1711, 1718, 1722, 1729, and 1733: Adam./ EDyce; Clowne. ABCDF
1722: you. / EDycel --, ABC; -- DG(5); --. -E

I am readie. And with this cudgell I will coniure thee.   1730

Diuell.

Oh hold thy hand, thou kilst me, thou kilst me.

Adam.

Then may I count my selfe I thinke a tall man, that am

able to kill a diuell. Now who dare deale with me in the

parish, or what wench in Niniuie will not loue me, when   1735

they say, there goes he that beate the diuell. $\lceil$ Exit. $\rfloor$

$\lceil$ IV, v $\rfloor$

Enter Thrasibulus.

Thrasi.

Loathed is the life that now inforc'd I leade,

But since necessitie will haue it so,

(Necessitie it doth command the Gods)

Through euerie coast and corner now I prie,   1740

To pilfer what I can to buy me meate.

Here haue I got a cloake not ouer old,

Which will afford some little sustenance,

Now will I to the broaking Vsurer,

To make exchange of ware for readie coine.   1745

$\lceil$ Enter Alcon, Samia, and Clesiphon. $\rfloor$

Alcon.

Wife bid the Trumpets sound a prize, a prize, mark

1736: $\lceil$ Exit. $\rfloor$/ EF; $\lceil$ Exit. Dyce; omitted ABCD
1745-46: $\lceil$ Enter Alcon, Samia, and Clesiphon. $\rfloor$/ EF; omitted ABCD;
       Enter ALCON, SAMIA, and CLESIPHON. Dyce

the posie, I cut t his from a new married wife, by the

helpe of a horne thombe and a knife, size shillings four

pence.

Samia.

The better lucke ours, but what haue we heare, cast

apparell. Come away man, the Vsurer is neare, this

is dead ware, let it not bide on our hands.   1750

Thrasi.

Here are my partners in my pouertie,

Inforc'd to seeke their fortunes as I do.

Ah-lasse that fewe men should possesse the wealth,

And many soules be forc'd to beg or steale.   1755

Alcon well met.

Alcon.

Fellow begger whither now?

Thrasi.

To the Vsurer to get gold on commoditie.

Alcon.

And I to the same place to get a vent for my villany,

see where the olde crust comes, let vs salute him, God

speede sir may a man abuse your patience vpon a pawune.   1760

Diuell. /

Vsurer.

Friend let me see it.   G4

Alcon.

Ecce signum, a faire doublet and hose, new brought out

of the pilferers shop, a hansome cloake.

Vsurer.

How were they gotten? 1765

Thrasi.

How catch the fisher-men fish? Master take them as you
thinke them worth, we leaue all to your conscience.

Vsurer.

Honest men, toward men, good men, my friends, like to
proue good members, vse me, command me, I will maintaine
your credits, there's mony, now spend not your time in
idlenesse, bring me commoditie I haue crownes for you, 1770
there is two shillings for thee, and six shillings for
thee.

Alcon.

A bargaine, now Samia haue at it for a new smocke, come
let vs to the spring of the best liquor, whilest this
lastes, tril-lill. 1775

Vsurer.

Good fellowes, propper fellowes, my companions, farwell,
I haue a pot for you.

Samia.

If he could spare it.

      Enters to them Ionas.

⌐ Ionas. ⌐

———————————

1780: ⌐ Ionas. ⌐/ EF; omitted ABCD; JONAS. Dyce

Repent you men of Niniuie, repent,   1780

The day of horror and of torment comes,

When greedie hearts shall glutted be with fire,

When as corruptions vailde, shall be unmaskt,

When briberies shall be repaide with bane,

When whoredomes shall be recompenc'd in hell,   1785

When riot shall with regor be rewarded,

When as neglect of truth, contempt of God,

Disdaine of poore men, fatherlesse and sicke,

Shall be rewarded with a bitter plague.

Repent ye men of Niniuie, repent.   1790

The Lord hath spoke, and I do crie it out.

There are as yet but fortie daies remaining,

And then shall Niniuie be ouerthrowne.

Repent ye men of Niniuie, repent.

There are as yet but fortie daies remaining,   1795

And then shall Niniuie be ouerthrowne. ⌐ Exit. /

Vsur.

Confus'd in thought, oh whither shall I wend? ⌐ Exit.   G4v

Thrasi.

My conscience cries that I haue done amisse. ⌐ Exit.

Alcon.

Oh God of heauen, gainst thee haue I offended. ⌐ Exit.

1784: bane, / EFDyce; --. ABCD
1785: hell, / EFDycel --. ABCD
1786: rewarded, / EFDyce; --. ABCD
1796, 1797, 1798, 1799, 1800, and 1803: ⌐ Exit./ BEFG(2); Exet. ACD;
    Exit. Dyce

Samia.

Ashamed of my misdeeds, where shal I hide me? ⁄ Exit. 1800

Clesi.

Father methinks this word repent is good,

He that punisheth disobedience,

Doth hold a scourge for euery priuie fault. ⁄ Exit.

Oseas.

Looke London, look, with inward eies behold,

What lessons the euents do here vnfold. 1805

Sinne growne to pride, to misery is thrall,

The warning bell is rung, beware to fall.

Ye worldy men whom wealth doth lift on hie,

Beware and feare, for wordly men must die.

The time shall come, where least suspect remaines, 1810

The sword shall light vpon the wisest braines.

The head that deemes to ouer-top the skie,

Shall perish in his humaine pollicie.

Lo I haue said, when I haue said the truth,

When will is law, when folly guideth youth, 1815

When shew of zeale is prankt in robes of zeale,

When Ministers powle the pride of common-weale,

When law is made a laborinth of strife,

When honour yeelds him friend to wicked life,

When Princes heare by others eares their follie,   1820

When vsury is most accounted holie,

If these shall hap, as would to God they might not,

The plague is neare; I speake although I write not.

      Enters the Angell.

Angell. Oseas.   1825

Oseas. Lord.

Angell.

Now hath thine eies perus'd these hainous sins,

Hateful vnto the mightie Lord of hostes,

The time is come, their sinnes are waxen ripe,

And though the Lord forewarnes, yet they repent not: /   1830

Custome of sinne hath hardned all their hearts,   H1

Now comes reuenge armed with mightie plagues,

To punish all that liue in Niniuie,

For God is iust as he is mercifull,

And doubtlesse plagues all such as scorne repent,   1835

Thou shalt not see the desolation

That falles vnto these cursed Niniuites,

But shalt returne to great Ierusalem,

And preach vnto the people of thy God,

What mightie plagues are incident to sinne,   1840

Vnlesse repentance mittigate his ire:

Wrapt in the spirit as thou wert hither brought,

1821: holie, / FDyce; --. ABCD; --; E
1823: neare; / EFG(Dyce); --, ABCD

Ile seate thee in <u>Iudeas</u> prouinces,

Feare not Oseas then to preach the word.

<u>Oseas.</u>

The <u>will</u> <u>of</u> <u>the</u> <u>Lord</u> be done.   1845

Oseas taken away.

<u>[</u> V, i <u>]</u>

<u>Enters</u> <u>Rasni</u> <u>with</u> <u>his</u> <u>Viceroyes,</u> <u>Aluida</u> <u>and</u> <u>her</u> <u>Ladies,</u>
to a banquet.

<u>Rasni.</u>

So Viceroyes you haue pleased me passing well,

These curious cates are gratious in mine eye.   1850

But these Borachios of the richest wine,

Make me to thinke how blythsome we will be.

Seate thee faire <u>Iuno</u> in the royall throne,

And I will serue thee to see thy face,

That feeding on the beautie of thy lookes,   1855

My stomache and mine eyes may both be fild.

Come lordings seate you, fellow mates at feast,

And frolicke wags, this is a day of glee,

This banquet is for brightsome <u>Aluida.</u>

Ile haue them skinch my standing bowles with wine,   1860

And no man drinke, but quaffe a whole carowse,

Vnto the health of beautious <u>Aluida.</u>

For who so riseth from this feast not drunke,

1851: Borachios / borachios <u>Dyce</u>; <u>Borachins</u> G(4); Borachious <u>ABCD</u>

As I am Rasni Niniuies great king,

Shall die the death as traitor to my selfe, /   1865

For that he scornes the health of Aluida.   H1v

K. Cili.

That will I neuer do my Lord.

Therefore with fauour, fortune to your grace,

Carowse vnto the health of Aluida.

Rasni.

Gramercy Lording, here I take thy pleadge.   1870

And Creete to thee a bowle of Greekish wine,

Here to the health of Aluida.

Creete.

Let come my Lord, Jack scincker fil it full,

A pleadge vnto the health of heauenly Aluida.

Rasni.

Vassals attendant on our royall feasts,   1875

Drinke you I say vnto my louers health,

Let none that is in Rasnies royall court,

Go this night safe and sober to his bed.

    Enters ⌐ Adam, ⌐ the Clowne.

Adam.

This way he is, and here will I speake with him.   1880

Lord.

1871; 1873: Creete / See the Commentary.
1877: Rasnies / CDG(3-5); Rasnes AB; Rasnis EF; Rasni's Dyce
1879, 1880, 1882, 1886: ⌐ Adam, ⌐ the Clowne. / EDyce; Clowne. ABCDF

Fellow, whither pressest thou?

Adam.

I presse no bodie sir, I am going to speake with a
friend of mine.

Lord.

Why slaue, here is none but the King and his Viceroyes.   1885

Adam.

The King, marry sir he is the man I would speake withall.

Lord.

Why calst him a friend of thine?

Adam.

I marry do I sir, for if he be not my friend, ile make
him my friend ere he and I passe.   1890

Lord.

Away vassaile be gone, thou speake vnto the King.

Adam.

I marry will I sir, and if he were a king of veluet,
I will talke to him.

Rasni.

Whats the matter there, what noyce is that?

Adam.

A boone my Liege, a boone my Liege.   1895

Rasni.

What is it that great Rasni will not graunt

1884: slaue, / BCDEFG(2-5)Dyce; flaue, A

This day, vnto the meanest of his land?

In honour of his beautious <u>Aluida</u>?

Come hither swaine, what is it that hou crauest?

Adam.

Faith sir nothing, but to speake a fewe sentences to
your worship. /

Rasni.

Say, what is it?

Adam.

I am sure sir you haue heard of the spirits that walke
in the Citie here.

Rasni.

I, what of that?

Adam.

Truly sir, I haue an oration to tel you of one of them
and this it is.

Alui.

Why goest not forward with thy tale?

Adam.

Faith mistresse, I feele an imperfection in my voyce,
a disease that often troubles me, but alasse easily
mended, a cup of Ale, or a cup of wine, will serue the
turne.

1900

H2

1905

1910

1889, 1892, 1895, 1900, 1903, 1906, 1908: Adam./ E<u>Dyce</u>; <u>Clowne</u>. ABCDF
1902: <u>Rasni</u>./ BCDEFG(2-5,Dyce)Dyce; --, A

Alui.

Fill him a bowle, and let him want no drinke.

Adam.

Oh what a pretious word was that, and let him want
no drinke. Well sir, now ile tel you foorth my tale:
Sir as I was comming alongst the port ryuale of Niniuie,   1915
there appeared to me a great diuell, and as hard
fauoured a diuell as euer I saw: nay sir, he was a
cuckoldly diuell, for he had hornes on his head. This
diuell, marke you now, presseth vpon me, and sir indeed,
I charged him with my pike staffe, but when that would
not serue, I came vpon him with spiritus santus, why   1920
it had bene able to haue put Lucifer out of his wits,
when I saw my charme would not serue, I was in such
a perplexitie, that sixe peny-worth of Iuniper would
not haue made the place sweete againe.

Alui.

Why fellow weart thou so afraid?

Adam.

Oh mistresse had your bene there and seene, his verie   1925
sight had made you shift a cleane smocke, I promise
you though I were a man and counted a tall fellow,

1912, 1925, 1931, and 1934: Adam. / EDyce; Clowne. ABCDF
1915: port royal / G(Dyce); port ryale AB; port ryalt CG(3,4); port-
    Ryale DEG(5)
1920: spiritus santus: / C; sprytus santus. ABD; sprytus santus - EF

yet my Landresse calde me slouenly knaue the next day.

Rasni.

A pleasaunt slaue, forward sirrha, on with thy tale.   1930

Adam.

Faith sir, but I remember a word that my mistresse
your bed fellow spoake.

Rasni.

What was that fellow?

Adam.

Oh sir, a word of comfort, a pertious word: and let
him want no drinke.   1935

Rasni.

Her word is lawe: and thou shalt want no drinke. /

Adam.

Then sir, this diuell came vpon me and would not be   H2v
perswaded but he would needs carry me to hell, I proffered
him a cup of Ale, thinking because he came out of so
hotte a place that he was thirstie, but the diuell   1940
was not drie, and therefore the more sorie was I,
well, there was no remedie but I must with him to
hell, and at last I cast mine eye aside, if you knew
what I spied you would laugh, sir I lookt from top
to toe, and he had no clouen feete. Then I ruffled
vp my haire, and set my cap on the one side, and sir   1945
grew to be a Iustice of peace to the diuel. At last

1937: Adam./ EDyce; Clowne. ABCDF

in a great fume, as I am very chollcricke, and
sometime so hotte in my fustian fumes that no man
can abide within twentie yards of me, I start vp,
and so bombasted the diuell, that sir he cried out,
and ranne away.   1950

Alui.

This plasant knaue hath made me laugh my fill.

Rasni, now Aluida begins her quaffe,

And drinkes a full carouse vnto her King.

Rasni.

A pleadge my loue, as hardie as great Ioue,

Drunke, when his Iuno heau'd a bowle to him.   1955

Frolicke my Lords, let all the standerds walke.

Ply it till euery man hath tane his lcad.

How now sirrha, what cheere, we haue no words of you.

Adam.

Truly sir, I was in a broune study about my mistresse.

Alui.

About me for what?   1960

Adam.

Truly mistresse, to thinke what a golden sentence you
did speake: all the philosophers in the world could not

1948: fustian / EFG(Dyce); fastin A; fustin BCG(2-4) fusten DG(5)
1954: hartie / BCDEFG(2-5,Dyce); hardie A
1956: Lords; / EFG(Dyce); Lord, ABCD
1958: what / BCDEFG(2-5,Dyce); how A
1959, 1961, 1974: Adam. / EDyce; Clowne. ABCLF

haue said more; what, come, let him want no drinke.

Oh wise speech.

Alui.

Villaines why skinck you not vnto this fellow?

He makes me blyth and merry in my thoughts.   1965

Heard you not that the King hath giuen command,

That all be drunke this day within his Court,

In quaffing to the health of Aluida?

        Enters Ionas.

Ionas.

Repent, repent, ye men of Niniuie repent.   1970

The Lord hath spoken, and I do crie it out,

There are as yet but fortie daies remaining,

And then shall Niniuie be ouerthrowne. /

Repent ye men of Niniuie, repent.   H3

Rasni.

What fellow is this, that thus disturbes our feasts,   1975

With outcries and alarums to repent.

Adam.

Oh sir, tis one goodman Ionas that is come from Iericho,

and surely I thinke he hath seene some spirit by the

way, and is fallen out of his wits, for he neuer leauies

crying night nor day, my maister heard him, and he shut

vp his shop, gaue me my Indenture, and he and his wife   1980

1963: what, come, / G(Dyce); 'what, come, ...' EF; what come ABCDG(2-5)
1976: alarums / CG(3-5)Dyce; alarums ABEF

do nothing but fast and pray.

Ionas.

Repent ye men of Niniuie, repent.

Rasni.

Come hither fellow, what art, and from whence commest

thou?

Ionas.

Rasni, I am a Prophet of the Lord,

Sent hither by the mightie God of hostes,   1985

To cry destruction to the Niniuites,

O Niniuie thou harlot of the world,

I raise thy neighbours round about thy boundes,

To come and see thy filthinesse and sinne.

Thus saith the Lord, the mightie God of hostes,   1990

Your King loues chambering and wantonnesse,

Whoredome and murther do distaine his Court,

He fauoureth couetous and drunken men.

Behold therefore all like a strumpet foule,

Thou shalt be iudg'd and punisht for thy crims: 1995

The foe shall pierce the gates with iron rampes,

The fire shall quite consume thee from aboue.

The houses shall be burnt, the Infants slaine.

And women shall behold their husbands die,

Thine eldest sister is Lamana.   2000

1990: hostes, / EF; hosts, DG(4,Dyce); hoste, AB
2000: Lamana./ See the Commentary.

And Sodome on thy right hand seated is.

Repent ye men of Niniuie, repent.

The Lord hath spoke, and I do crie it out.

There are as yet but fortie daies remaining,

And then shall Niniuie be ouerthrowne.   2005

Exit.

Rasni.

Staie Prophet, staie.

Ionas.

Disturbe not him that sent me,

Let me performe the message of the Lord. Exit. /

Rasni.

My soule is buried in the hell of thoughts.   2010   H3v

Ah Aluida, I looke on thee with shame.

My Lords on sodeine fixe their eyes on ground,

As if dismayd to looke vpon the heauens.

Hence Magi, who haue flattered me in sinne.

Exit. His sages.   2015

Horror of minde, disturbance of my soule,

Make me agast, for Niniuies mishap.

Lords see proclaim'd, yea see it straight proclaim'd,

That man and beast, the woman and her childe,

2006: Exit. / CDEF; Exet offered. ABG(2,5); ⌐ Exit offered. Dyce
2009: Exit. / BCDEFG(2); Ext. A; ⌐ Exit. Dyce
2015: Exit. His sages. / BG(2); Exet. His sages. A; Exit. his sages.
    CG(3,4); Exit sages. DG(5); Exeunt his Exeunt Magi. F
2017: Make / EDyce; Makes ABCDF

For fortie daies in sacke and ashes fast,   2020

Perhaps the Lord will yeeld and pittie vs.

Beare hence these wretched blandishments of sinne,

And bring me sackcloth to attire your King.

/ Taking off his crown and robe.

Away with pompe, my soule is full of woe:

In pittie looke on Niniuie, O God.   2025

Exit a man

Alui.

Assaild with shame, with horror ouerborne,

To sorrowes sold, all guiltie of our sinne.

Come Ladies come, let vs prepare to pray.

Ah-lasse, how dare we looke on heauenly light,   2030

That haue dispisde the maker of the same?

How may we hope for mercie from aboue,

That still dispise the warnings from aboue?

Woes me, my conscience is a heauie foe.

O patron of the poore opprest with sinne,   2035

Looke, looke on me, that now for pittie craue,

Assaild with shame, with horror ouerborne,

To sorrow sold, all guiltie of our sinne.

Come Ladies come, let vs prepare to pray.

Exeunt.   2040

2023: / Taking off his crown and robe. 7 / EF; omitted ABCDDyce
2026: Exit a man. / Dyce; Exit. A man BFG(2); Exet. A man. A; Exit. A man.
CG(3,4); Exit. DG(5); / Exeunt and except Aluida and Ladies. E

_ V, ii _7

Enter the Vsurer solus, with a halter in one

    hand, a dagger in the other.

Vsurer.

Groning in conscience, burdened with my crimes,

The hell of sorrow hauntes me vp and downe. /

Tread where I lift, mee-thinkes the bleeding ghostes,   2045   H4

Of those whom my corruption brought to noughts,

Do serue for stumbling blocks before my steppes.

The fatherlesse and widow wrongd by me,

The poore oppressed by my vsurie,

Mee-thinkes I see their hands read vp to heauen,   2050

To crie for vengeance of my couetousnesse.

Where so I walke, Ile sigh and shunne my way.

Thus am I made a monster of the world,

Hell gapes for me, heauen will not hold my soule.

You mountaines shoude me from the God of truth.   2055

Mee-thinkes I see him sit to iudge the earth.

See how he blots me out of the booke of life.

Oh burthen more then Atna that I beare.

Couer me hilles, and shroude me from the Lord.

Swallow me Licas, shield me from the Lord.   2060

In life no peace: each murmuring that I heare,

Mee-thinkes the sentence of damnation soundes,

1048: me, / CEFG(3-5)Dyce; --. AB

Die reprobate, and hie thee hence to hell.

    The <u>euill angell</u> tempteth <u>him</u>, offering

        the <u>knife and</u> rope.   2065

What fiend is this that temptes me to the death?

What is my death the harbour of my rest?

Then let me die: what second charge is this?

Mee-thinks I heare a voice amidst mine eares,

That bids me staie: and tels me that the Lord   2070

Is mercifull to those that do repent.

May I repent? oh thou my doubtfull soule?

Thou maist repent, the Iudge is mercifull.

Hence tooles of wrath, stales of temptation,

For I will pray and sign vnto the Lord.   2075

In sackcloth will I sigh, and fasting pray:

O Lord in rigor looke not on my sinnes.

<u>He sits him downe in</u> sack-cloathes, <u>his hands</u>

    <u>and eyes reared to heauen.</u>/

<u>Enters Aluida with her Ladies, with dispiearsed locks.</u>   2080

<u>Alui.</u>

Come mournfull dames laie off your brodred locks,

And on your shoulders spread dispiearsed haires,

Let voice of musicke cease, where sorrow dwels.

Cloathed in sackcloaths, sigh your sinnes with me.

2068: Then / CDEFG(3-5)Dyce; Theu ABG(2)
2069: Mee-thinks / DEF; Mee-things A; Meethinke, BG(2); Mee-thinkes CG(3);
    Methinks Dyce
2080: locks./ EDyce; locks, F; lookes ABCD

Bemone your pride, bewaile your lawlesse lusts,   2085 **H4v**

With fasting mortifie your pampered loines:

Oh thinke vpon the horrour of your sinnes.

Think, think, with me, the burthen of your blames,

Woe to thy pompe, false beautie, fading floure,

Blasted by age, by sicknesse, and by death.   2090

Woe to our painted cheekes, our curious oyles,

Our rich array, that fostered vs in sinne.

Woe to our idle thoughts that wound our soules.

Oh would to God all nations might receiue,

A good example by our greeuous fall.   2095

Ladies.

You that are planted there where pleasure dwels,

And thinke your pompe as great as Niniuies,

May fall for sinne as Niniuie doth now.

Alui.

Mourne, mourne, let moane be all your melodie,

And pray withe me, and I will pray for all.   2100

O Lord of heauen forgiue vs our misdeeds.

Ladies.

O Lord of heauen forgiue vs our misdeeds.

Vsurer.

O Lord of light forgiue me my misdeeds.

2089: false / EFG(Dyce); fall CG(3,4); --, BDG(2,5); Ful, e A
2097: think / G(Dyce); thinkes ABCDEF
2101: omitted / EFDyce; Lord. ABD; Lords. CG(3,4) See the Commentary.

Enter Rasni, the King of Assiria, with his nobles

in sackcloath.   2105

K. Cilicia.

Be not so ouercome with grieffe O King,

Least you endanger life by sorrowing so.

Rasni.

King of Cilicia, should I cease my griefe,

Where as my swarming sinne afflict my soule?

Vaine man know, this my burthen greater is,   2110

Then euery priuate subiect's in my land:

My life hath bene a loadstarre vnto them,

To guide them in the laborinth of blame,

Thus I haue taught them for to do amisse: /

Then must I weepe my friend for their amisse,   2115   Il

The fall of Niniuie is wrought by me:

I haue maintaind this Citie in her shame.

I haue contemn'd the warnings from aboue.

I haue vpholden incest, rape, and spoyle.

Tis I that wrought the sinne, must weepe the sinne.   2120

Oh had I teares like to the siluer streames,

That from the Alpine Mountains sweetly streame,

Oh had I sighes the treasures of remorse,

As plentifull as Aeolus hath blasts,

I then would tempt the heauens with my laments,   2125

2104: King / BCDEFLyce; Kings A
2111: subiect's / G(Lyce); subject(s) E; subiect ABCDF

And piece the throane of mercy by my sighes.

K. Cil.

Heauens are propitious vnto faithful praiers.

Rasni.

But after our repent, we must lament:

Least that a worser mischiefe doth befall.

Oh pray, perhaps the Lord will pitie vs.   2130

Oh God of truth both mercifull and iust,

Behold repentant men with pitious eyes,

We waile the life that we haue led before.

O pardon Lord, O pitie Niniuie.   2135

Rasni.

Let not the Infants dallying on the teat,

For fathers sinnes in iudgement be opprest.

K. Cil.

Let not the painfull mothers big with childe,

The innocents be punisht for our sinne.

Rasni. O pardon Lord, O pitie Niniuie.   2140

Omnes. O pardon Lord, O pitie Niniuie.

Rasni.

O Lord of heauen, the virgins weepe to thee.

The couetous man is sorie for his sinne.

The Prince and poore, all pray before thy throane.

2127: propitious / CEFG(3)Dyce; prepitious ABD
2136: teat, / CEFG(3,4)Dyce; tent ABD
2143: is sorie / sorie BCDG(2,5); sorie sorie A; sorrie E; sore sorie F;
     sorry G(Dyce)Dyce

And wilt thou then be wroth with <u>Niniuie</u>?   2145

<u>K. Cili.</u>

Giue truce to praier O King, and rest a space.

<u>Rasni</u>.

Giue truce to praiers, when times require no truce?

No Princes no. Let all our subiects hie

Vnto our temples, where on humbled knees,

I will expect some mercy from aboue.   2150

<u>Enter</u> the <u>temple</u> <u>Omnes.</u>

<u>Enter</u> <u>Ionas</u>, <u>solus.</u>

$\int$ V, iii $\rfloor$

<u>Ionas.</u>

This is the day wherein the Lord hath said /

That <u>Niniuie</u> shall quite be ouerthrowne.   I1v

This is the day of horrow and mishap,

Fatall vnto the cursed <u>Niniuites</u>.   2155

These stately Towers shall in thy watery bounds,

Swift flowing <u>Licas</u> find their burials,

These pallaces the pride of <u>Assurs</u> kings,

Shall be the bowers of desolation,

Where as the sollitary bird shall sing,   2160

And Tygers traine their yoong ones to'ther nest.

O all ye nations bounded by the West,

Ye happie Iles where Prophets do abound,

2150: expect / <u>CDFDyce</u>; exspect <u>ABE</u>

Ye Cities famous in the western world,

Make Niniuie a president for you.   2165

Leaue leaud desires, leaue ccuetous delights.

Flie vsurie, let whoredome be exilde,

Least you with Niniuie be ouerthrowne.

Loe how the sunnes inflamed torch preuailes,

Scorching the parched furrowes of the earth.   2170

Here will I sit me downe and fixe mine eye

Vpon the ruines of yon wretched towne,

And lo a pleasant shade, a spreading vine,

To shelter Ionas in this sunny heate!

What meanes my God, the day is done and spent.   2175

Lord shall my Prophecie be brought to nought?

When falles the fire? when will the iudge be wroth?

I pray thee Lord remember what I said,

When I was yet within my country land,

Iehouah is too mercifull I feare.   2180

O let me flie before a Prophet fault,

For thou art mercifull the Lord my God,

Full of compassion and of sufferance,

And doest repent in taking punishment.

Why staies thy hand? O Lord first take my life,   2185

Before my Prophesie be brought to nought.

Ah he is wroth, behold the gladsome vine

2174: heate! / CFG(3,4)Dyce; --, AB; --. DE
2186: nought. / CG(3,4); noughts. ABDEF; noughts! Dyce

That did defend me from the sunny heate,

Is withered quite, and swallowed by a Serpent.

A Serpent deuoureth the vine. /   2190

Now furious Phlegon triumphs on my browes,   I2

And heate preuailes, and I am faint in heart.

Enters the Angell.

Angell.

Art thou so angry Ionas? tell me why?

Ionas.

Iehouah I with burning heate am plungde,   2195

And shadowed only by a silly vine,

Behold a Serpent hath deuoured it:

And lo the sunne incenst by Easterne winde,

Afflicts me with canicular aspect,

Would God that I might die, for well I wot,   2200

Twere better I were dead, then rest aliue.

Angell.

Ionas art thou so angry for the vine?

Ionas.

Yea I am angry to the death my God.

Angell.

Thou hast compassion Ionas on a vine,

On which thou neuer labour diast bestow,   2205

Thou neuer gauest it life or power to grow,

2197: it:/CFG(3,4)Dyce; --? AE; --. BDG(2-5)
2199: canicular / EFG(Dyce)Dyce; Canicular F; Caricular ABCD

But sodeinly it sprung, and sodeinly dide.

And should not I haue great compassion

On Niniuie the Citie of the world,

Wherein there are a hundred thousand soules,   2210

And twentie thousand infants that ne wot

The right hand from the left, beside much cattle.

Oh Ionas, looke into their Temples now,

And see the true contrition of their King:

The subiects teares, the sinners true remorse.   2215

Then from the Lord proclaime a mercie day,

For he is pitifull as he is iust. Exit Angelus.

Ionas.

I go my God to finish they command,

Oh who can tell the wonders of my God,   2220

Or talke his praises with a seruent toong?

He bringeth downe to hell, and lifts to heauen.

He drawes the yoake of bondage from the iust,

And lookes vpon the Heathen with pitious eyes:

To him all praise and honour be ascribed.   2225

Oh who can tell the wonders of my God,

He makes the infant t o proclaime his truth, /

The Asse to speake, to saue the Prophets life,   I2v

The earth and sea to yeeld increase for man.

2218: Exit Angelus. / BCDFG(2); Exet. AE; ⌐ Exit Angelus. Dyce
2221: toong? / CF; --. AB; tongue. D; tong? F; tongue? Dyce
2228: life, / EFDyce --. ABCD; --G(Ḻ)

Who can describe the compasse of his power?   2230

Or testifie in termes his endlesse might?

My rauisht spright, oh whither doest thou wend?

Go and proclaime the mercy of my God.

Relieue the carefull hearted <u>Niniuites</u>.

And as thou weart the messenger of death,   2235

Go bring glad tydings of recouered grace. ⎣ <u>Exit</u>.

Enters <u>Adam solus, with a bottle of beere in one</u>

<u>slop, and a great peece of beefe in an other</u>.

⎣ V, iv ⎦

⎣ <u>Adam</u>. ⎦

Well good-man <u>Ionas</u>, I would you had neuer come from

<u>Iury</u> to this Country, you haue made me looke like a   2240

leane rib of roast beefe, or like the picture of

lent, painted vpon a read-herings cob. Alasse

maisters, we are commanded by the proclamation to

fast and pray, by my troth I could prettely so, so,

away with praying, but for fasting, why tis so

contrary to my nature, that I had rather suffer a short

hanging, then a long fasting. Marke me, the words be   2245

these. Thou shalt take no maner of foode for so

many daies. I had as leeue he should haue said,

thou shalt hang thy selfe for so many daies, And yet

2236: ⎣ <u>Exit</u>. / EFDyce; omitted ABCD
2239: ⎣ <u>Adam</u>. ⎦ / E; ⎣ <u>Clowne</u>. ⎦ F; omitted ABCD

in faith I need not finde fault with the proclamation,   2250

for proofe, Ecce signum, this right slop is my pantry,

behold a manchet, this place is my kitchen, for loe

a peece of beefe. Oh let me repeat that sweet word

againe: For loe a peece of beef. This is my buttry,

for see, see, my friends, to my great ioy, a bottle

of beere. Thus alasse I make shift to weare out this

fasting, I driue away the time, but there go Searchers   2255

about to seeke if any man breakes the Kings command.

Oh here they be, in with your victuals Adam.

                    Enter two Searchers.

I. Searcher.

How duly the men of Niniuie keep the proclamation,

how are they armde to repentance? we haue searcht   2260

through the whole Citie and haue not as yet found one

that breaks the fast.

2. Sear.

The signe of the more grace, but staie, here sits

one mee-thinkes at his praiers, let vs see who it is.

I. Sear.

Tis Adam, the Smithes man, how now Adam?

Adam.

Trouble me not, thou shalt take no maner of foode,

but /   2265

_____

2258: Enter / CG(3,4)Dyce; Enters ABDEF

fast and pray. 13

I. Sear.

How deuoutly he sits at his orysons, but staie,
mee-thinkes I feele a smell of some meate or bread
about him.

2. Sear.

So thinkes me too, you sirrha, what victuals haue you
about you ? 2270

Adam.

Victuals! Oh horrible blasphemie! Hinder me not
of my praier, nor driue me not into a chollor,
victuales! why hardst thou not the sentence, thou
shalt take no foode but fast and pray?

2. Sear.

Truth so it should be, but me-thinkes I smell meate
about thee. 2275

Adam.

About me my friends, these words are actions in the
Case, about me, No, no: hang those gluttons that
cannot fast and pray.

I. Sear.

Well, for all your words, we must search you.

Adam.

Search me, take heed what you do, my hose are my 2280
castles, tis burglary if you breake ope a slop, no
officer must lift vp an iron hatch, take heede my

slops are iron.

2. Sear.

Oh villaine, see how he hath gotten victuales, bread,
beefe, and beere, where the King commanded vpon paine
of death none should eate for so many daies, no not
the sucking infant.   2285

Adam.

Alasse sir, this is nothing but a modicum non cocet
ut medicus daret, why sir, a bit to comfort my stomache.

I. Sear.

Villaine thou shalt be hangd for it.

Adam.

These are your words, I shall be hangd for it, but
first answer me to this question, how many daies haue
we to fast stil?   2290

2. Sear. Fiue daies.

Adam.

Fiue daies, a long time, then I must be hangd?

I. Sear. I marry must thou.

Adam.

I am your man, I am for you sir, for I had rather be
hangd than abide so long a fast, what fiue daies? come
ile vntrusse, is your halter and the gallowes, the   2295
ladder, and all such furniture in readinesse?

2286: nocet / EFG(5)Dyce; necet ABC; necet, D

I. Sear.

I warrant thee, thou shalt want none of these.

Adam. But heare you, must I be hangd?

I. Sear. I marry.   2300

Adam.

And for eating of meate, then friends, know ye by
these presents, I will eate vp all my meate, and
drink vp all my drink, for it shall neuer be said, I
was hangd with an emptie stomake. /

I. Sear.

Come away knaue, wilt thou stand feeding now?   I3v

Adam.

If you be so hastie, hang your selfe an houre while   2305
I come to you, for surely I will eate vp my meate.

2. Sear.

Come lets draw him away perforce.

Adam.

You say there is fiue daies yet to fast, these are
your words.

2. Sear. I sir.

Adam.

I am for you, come lets away, and yet let me be put in
the Chronicles.   ⌐ Exeunt.   2310

_____

2298: thou shalt / DE; shalt ABCFDyce
2310: ⌐ Exeunt. / CEFDyce; omitted ABD

$\underline{\diagup}$ V, v $\underline{\diagdown}$

<u>Enter</u> <u>Ionas</u>, <u>Rasni</u>, <u>Aluida</u>, <u>King</u> <u>of</u> <u>Cilicia</u>, <u>others</u>
<u>royally</u> attended

<u>Ionas</u>.

Come carefull King, cast off thy mournfull weedes,

Exchange thy cloudie lookes to smothed smiles,

Thy teares haue pierc'd the pitious throane of grace,   2315

Thy sighes like <u>incense</u> pleasing to the Lord,

Haue bene peace-offerings for thy former pride.

Reioyce and praise his name that gaue thee peace.

And you faire <u>Nymphs</u>, ye louely <u>Niniuites</u>,

Since you haue wept and fasted for the Lord,   2320

He gratiously hath tempered his reuenge,

Beware hencefoorth to tempt him any more,

Let not the nicenesse of your beautious lookes,

Ingraft in you a high presuming minde,

For those that climbe, he casteth to the ground,   2325

And they that humble be, he lifts aloft.

<u>Rasni</u>.

Lowly I bend with awfull bent of eye,

Before the dread <u>Iehouah</u>, God of hostes,

Despising all prophane deuice of man,

2312: King / CDEFG(3-5)Dyce; Kings AB
2316: incense / EFG(Dyce)Dyce; Imence ABCD
2316: Lord, / CEFG(3,4)Dyce; --: ABD
2321: hath / DEFG(4,5)Dyce; haue ABC
2328: hostes, / F; hosts, EDyce; hoste, ABCD

Those lustfull lures that whilome led awry,   2330
My wanton eyes shall wound my heart no more:
And she whose youth in dalliance I abus'd,
Shall now at last become my wedlocke mate.
Faire <u>Aluida</u> looke not so woe begone:
If for thy sinne thy sorrow do exceed,   2335
Blessed be thou, come with a holy band,
Lets knit a knot to salue our former shame.

<u>Alui</u>.

With blushing lookes betokening my remorse,
I lowly yeeld my King to thy behest,
So as this man of God shall thinke it good.   2340

<u>Ionas</u>.

Woman, amends may neuer come too late. /
A will to practise good is vertuous.   14
The God of heauen when sinners do repent,
Doth more reioyce then in ten thousand iust.

<u>Rasni</u>.

Then witnesse holie Prophet our accord.   2345

<u>Alui</u>.

Plight in the presence of the Lord thy God.

<u>Ionas</u>.

Best may you be, like to the flouring sheaues,

2342: A will to practise good id vertuous. / <u>EFDyce</u>; A will to practise
    goodnesse virtuous <u>A</u>; I will thou practise goodnesse and
    vertuousnesse <u>BCDG(2-5)</u>

That plaie with gentle windes in sommer tide,

Like Oliue branches let your children spred:

And as the Pines in loftie Libanon,   2350

Or as the kids that feede on Lepher plaines,

So be the seede and offspring of your loines.

    Enters the Vsurer, Thrasibulus, and Alcon.

Vsurer.

Come foorth my friends whom wittingly I wrongd,

Before this man of God receiue your due,   2355

Ionas behold in signe of my remorse,

I neare restore into these poore means hands,

Their goods which I vniustly haue detaind,

And may the heauens so pardon my misdeeds,   2360

As I am penitent for my offence.

Thrasi.

And what through want from others I purloynd,

Behold O King, I proffer fore thy throane:

To be restord to such as owe the same.

Ionas.

A vertuous deed pleasing to God and man,   2365

Would God all Cities drowned in like shame,

Would take example of these Niniuites.

Rasni.

Such be the fruites of Niniuies repent,

2353: Thrasibulus, / EFDyce; Gentleman, ABCD
2366: in / BCDEFG(2)Dyce; iu A

And such for euer may our dealings be,

That he that cald vs home in height of sinne,   2370

May smile to see our hartie penitence.

Viceroyes proclaime a fast vnto the Lord,

Let Israels God be honoured in our land.

Let all occasion of corruption die.

For who shall fault therein, shall suffer death.   2375

Beare witnesse God, of my vnfained zeale.

Come holie man, as thou shalt counsaile me,

My Court and Citie shall reformed be.

Exeunt ⌐ all but Ionas. ⌐ /

Ionas.

Wend on in peace, and prosecute this course,   2380   I4v

You Flanders on whom the milder aire

Doth swaetly breath the balme of kinde increase:

Whose lands are fatned with the deaw of heauen,

And made more fruitfull then Actean plaines,

You whom delitious pleasures dandle soft: 2385

Whose eyes are blinded with securitie,

Vnmaske your selues, cast error cleane aside.

O London, mayden of the mistresse Ile,

Wrapt in the foldes and swathing cloutes of shame:

In thee more sinnes then Niniuie contains,   2390

Contempt of God, dispight of reuerend age,

2379: Exeunt ⌐ all but Ionas. ⌐/ EF; ⌐ Exeunt all but JONAS. Dyce;
Exeunt. ABCD
2391: age, / CDEFG(3-5)Dyce; --. AB

Neglect of law, desire to wrong the poore,

Corruption, whordome, drunkennesse, and pride,

Swolne are thy browes with impudence and shame.

O proud adulterous glorie of the West,   2395

Thy neighbors burn, yet doest thou scare no fire.

Thy preachers crie, yet doest thou stop thine eares.

The larum rings, yet sleepest thou secure.

London awake, for feare the Lord doth frowne,

I set a looking Glasse before thine eyes,   2400

O turne, O turne, with weeping to the Lord,

And thinke the praiers and vertues of thy Queene,

Defer the plague which otherwise would fall.

Repent O London, least for thine offence,

Thy shepheard faile, whom mightie God preserue,   2405

That she may bide the pillar of his Church,

Against the stormes of Romich Antichrist:

The hand of mercy of ouershead her head,

And let all faithfull subiects say, Amen.

FINIS.

2392: poore, / EFDyce; --: ABCD; --; G(4)
2396: neighbors burn, / G(Dyce)Dyce; neighbor burns. ABCDF; neighbors
    burne, E
2399: doth / CG(3,4); do ABDEFDyce
2403: Defer / Dyce; Defers ABCDEF

IV. Commentary or Explanatory Notes

A List of Abbreviations and Reference Materials

CNLD: Cassell's New Latin Dictionary.

Collins: J. Churton Collins, ed., The Plays and Poems of Robert Greene (Oxford: Clarendon Press, 1905). Vol. I.

DB: Dictionary of the Bible.

DCM: Dictionary of Classical Mythology

DLL: Dictionary of Latin Literature

Dyce: Alexander Dyce, ed., The Dramatic Works of Robert Greene (London: William Pickering, 1831). Vol. I.

ECM: The Encyclopedia of Classical Mythology

Greg: W. W. Greg, ed., A Looking Glass for London and England By Thomas Lodge and Robert Greene 1594 (London: Malone Society, 1932).

Grosart: Alexander B. Grosart, ed., The Life and Complete Works in Prose and Verse of Robert Greene, M. A. (London: Printed for Private Circulation, 1881-1883). Vol. XIV.

Law: Rubert Adger Law, "A Looking Glass and the Scriptures," University of Texas Studies (1931), pp. 31-47.

ODEP: The Oxford Dictionary of English Proverbs

OED: Oxford English Dictionary

SDM: Short Dictionary of Mythology

177

Swaen: A. E. H. Swaen, "A Looking-Glass for London and
        England: Nutmegs and Ginger," Modern Language
        Review, XXXIII (July 1938), 404-405.

WBD: Webster's Biographical Dictionary

WGD: Webster's Geographical Dictionary

        For the Biblical analogy in the Commentary I employ-
ed the following reference materials:

The holie bible. [Bishops'Bible.]* Ann Arbor: University
        Microfilms, [n. d.]. Huntington Library copy, [1568].
        [STC 2099].

The Geneva Bible. Ann Arbor: University Microfilms,
        [n. d.], Huntington Library copy, [1561]. [STC 2095].

Margaret M. Cotham, "Greene and Lodge's A Looking-Glass
        for London and England, " Unpublished M. A. thesis,
        University of Texas, 1928.

Encyclopedic Dictionary of the Bible.

Harper's Topical Concordance.

The Interpreter's Dictionary of the Bible.

Nelson's Complete Concordance of the Revised Standard
Version Bible.

*All the biblical quotations are taken from the Bishops'
Bible.

[I, i]

1: Rasni, / According to my collation notes, A (1594)
    spelled Rasin four times and Rasins only three
    times, while it used Rasni 54 times, Rasnis (or
    Rasnies or Rasnes) eleven times. This contrast
    in spelling variations seems to reveal that the play-
    wrights intended to spell Rasni and Rasnis (or its
    variant spellings) rather than Rasin and Rasins.

1: Rasni, the King of Nineveh / He seems to represent
    the corrupt kingdom and commits incest and adultery
    in the play, but in the Bible he corresponds to the
    Assyrian king in Jonah III, 6, although the name
    King Rasni which the dramatists use is not mentioned
    at all.

1: Cilicia / In the Geneva Bible there is no mention of
    Cilicia, the King of which country is a more or
    less prominent figure throughout the Rasni scenes
    of the play. The name was possibly suggested by
    a marginal note on the opening page of Ionas in the
    Bishops' Bible, wherein we learn that Tharsis is
    "the name of a place likely to be Cilicia, for there
    was a great citie of that name where also Paul was
    borne" (Law, p. 37). See 1006 and 1008.

         Cilicia is "an ancient country and region in
    SE Asia Minor, extending along Mediterranean coast
    S. of Taurus Mts. from the Amanus Mts. to Pamphy-
    lia. As a modern region in Turkey, called also
    Lesser Armenia" (WGD).

         Cilicia is cited as the birthplace of Saul of
    Tarsus in Acts XXI, 39.

3: Jeroboam, the King of Jerusalem / Rasni has conquered
    him as the play opens. He is identified as King of
    Israel who was overthrown by Abijah, King of Judah,
    who "raigned three yeares in Hierusalem" (II
    Chronicles XIII, 2).

5: Lemmon / Lemon-Mars, a sweetheart or a lover
    (Collins; OED; Dyce).

6: hardy / bold or courageous (OED).

13: Lycus / King Rasni proudly asks: "Am I not he that
     rules great Niniuie, / Rounded with Lycas siluer
     flowing streams?" Later in 1497-98, Ionas exclaims
     on seeing Ninivie: "Behold sweete Licas streaming
     in his boundes, / Bearing the walles of haughtie
     Niniuie. " Collins notes on the first of these pass-
     ages as follows: "Many Asiatic rivers bore the
     name of Lycus, but none of them bounded or could
     bound Nineveh. Greene has evidently confounded
     the Lycus with the Tigris, on the left bank of which
     Nineveh is said to have been situated" (Collins, ed. ,
     I, 290). However, he failed to recognize the
     marginal gloss opposite the first verses of the Book
     of Ionas in the Bishops' Bible, which states that
     Ninivie is "the greatest citie of the Assyrians,
     situated by the riuer Lucus as Strabo writeth. "
     No such note is on the corresponding page of the
     Geneva Bible, nor any mention of Lycus. Thus,
     both the wording and the glosses of the Bishops'
     Bible point to the use by Lodge and Greene of that
     version rather than any other for details of the
     Ionas story (Law, pp. 37-38).

14-15: Whose Citie large Diametri containes, / Euen three
     daies iournies length from wall to wall, / seems to
     correspond to a Biblical passage, "So Jonas arose, and
     went to Niniuie according to the word of the Lord
     (Niniuie was a great citie and excellent, of three
     dayes iourney.)" (Jonah III, 3)

14: Dimetri / Diametrus (L.)=the length of a circle (OED).

16: burnished / polished or made bright and shining as by
     friction (OED).

17: portoyle / portrait (OED).

24: Judea / An ancient region in Palestine constituting
     the S. division (Judah) of the country under Persian,
     Greek, and Roman rule (WGD).

26: Cades=Cadis / a province of Spain; Kadesh in Vulgate,
     Gen. XX, i, Joshua, XII (Greg).

26: Samaria / Northern kingdom, Israel or modern Jordan;

district of ancient Palestine between the Mediterranean
and the Jordan S. of Galilee and N. of Judea (WGD).

27: stout / strong in endurance or undaunted and vigorous
in conflict or resistance (OED).

27: Benhadad / the name of three kings of Damascus;
Benhadad, or Benhadab, but unrevised Vulgate, III,
Kings XV, 18, Benadab (Greg).

28: rebate / to reduce the force of or to diminish (OED).

34: bane / woe (Dyce); ruin or the cause of death (OED).

36: Nunpareile / no parallel (i. e., non pareil) (Greg).

41: disparagement / lowering of value, honour or estimation
(OED).

42: daughtie / capable; virtuous; brave; formidable (OED).

44: Curtelex=curtel-axe / a short broad cutting sword
(OED).

48: Pallas / Another name for Athena (DCM); a name of
Minerva given to her because she slew a famous
giant of that name (SDM).

51: Dania=Diana / the virgin goddess of the hunt and of
the moon. Sister of Apollo, identified with the
Greek Artemis (DLL).

54: tide / tied (Greg).

58: bringing / "bring" should be either "brings" in order
to agree to "Enters" or "bringing" in order to
function as a participial modifier.

62: stroyes=strows / raze, level, the primary sense
(Greg); (Dyce).

67: Aeolus=Aeolis or Aeolia / God of the winds (DCM).

79: Trull / a girl or a low prostitute; a lass (OED).

81: she that basht the sun-god with her eyes / either
Leucothea or Clytie (Collins); Leucothea=the name

of Ino after her transformation into a sea nymph;
Clytie=daughter of Oceanus and Tethys, beloved
of Apollo.   She had herself changed into a sun-
flower, in which metamorphosis turns constantly
towards Sol, or the sun god of Apollo.   (SDM).
See 548.

82:   Semele / in Greek mythology, a daughter of Cadmus
      and Harmonia.   Through Zeus she was the mother
      of Dionysus, and was slain by lightning when Zeus
      granted her request, appeared before her as the
      God of Thunder.   Sister of Agave, Autonoe, Ino,
      and Polydorus (DCM).

87:   fair / beauty (Dyce).

89:   For why / because (Collins).

97:   Diademe / a crown or royal or imperial dignity;
      sovereignty (OED).

101: prancke / to dress or deck in a gay, bright, or
      showy manner (OED).

106: Albia / Albion (Greg); Son of Neptune and Amphitrite,
      came to Britain where he established a kingdom,
      and introduced astrology, and the art of building
      ships (SDM).

106: Margarite / pearl (OED).

108: Tyre / a town S. Lebanon on the coast; ancient
      Phoenicia (WGD).

115: not sister to thy love / [take] not [thy] sister to thy
      love (Dyce); not sister to love (Collins).

118: presumptous / overstepping due bounds; impertinent;
      unduly bold or confident (OED).

119: twit / to taunt or to ridicule.

119: lowes / loues (Greg).

119: lowes? / to allow; or to praise.   It is also possible
      that "lowes" is "loues."   See the analogy: "two
      fowle" for "too foul" (116).

130: vicegerent / an administrative deputy of a king
      (OED).

134: quondam / sometime; former (OED).

157: Smith. / As Dyce notes in his 1831 edition, the
      Smith has not yet appeared. Rasni could have said
      this Latin phrase.

157: Divisum imperium Cum Ioue nunc teneo. / I share
      a kingdom now with Jove (or Now I hold a divided
      kingdom with Jove) (CNLD). This is an adaptation
      of the second line of the famous epigram attributed
      by Donatus to Virgil: "Nocte pluit tota; redeunt
      spectacula mane: / Divisum imperium cum Ioue
      Caesar habet" (Collins). *I am indebted to Dr.
      John L. Gribbem, a former Latin instructor, now
      an Associate Professor of English at Kent State
      University, for all the Latin translation in the
      Commentary.

[I, ii]

163: Elias=Elijah / a Hebrew prophet during the reigns
      of Ahab and Ahaziah of Israel (DB).

164: Carmell=Carmel / Mt. Carmel is a mountain ab.
      1800 ft. in NW Palestine near Mediterranean coast
      (WGD).

166: flintie=flinty / unyielding or stern (OED).

166-168: Whose flintie hearts haue felt no sweet remorse,
      But lightly valuing all the threats of God,
      Haue still perseuerd in their wickednesse /
      This seems to agree with the description of their
      stubbornness as given in the Bible by Hosea, who
      declares, "They wyll not geue their myndes to turne
      vnto their God" (Hosea V. 4).

168: perseuerd=persevere / to persist in a state (OED).

171: pampred=pampered / overindulged with what gratifies
      (OED).

173: Oseas asserts: The Lord lookes downe, and cannot
      see one good, / Compare Psalms, XV, 2-3 in the

Bishops' Bible: "God looked down from heauen
vpon the children of menne to / see if there were
any that did understand and seeke after God... /
There is none that dooth good, no not one" (Law,
p. 40).

175: cruch=crutch / a staff for a lame or infirm person
to lean upon in walking; a symbol of old age (OED).

190: Osea / Osea is Hosea in the Old Testament.

194: Smith / The speaker is the Smith's man, Adam, by
which name he is distinguished in the latter part of
the play (Dyce). See 771 and 1293.

199: paltrie / inferior, trashy, mean, despicable (OED).

215: Autem glorificam / I will also glorify (CNLD); there
is the same pun in Friar Bacon (Collins, II, 1.
1574), "But heres a nosethat I warrant may be
called nos autem propelare for the people of the
parish" (Collins).

220: that crost him ouer the thumbs / that brings under
his control (ODEP).

222: opproprious=opprobrious / infamous or disgraceful
(OED).

223: scabbard / the case or sheath which serves to protect the blade of a sword, dagger, or bayonet when
not in use (OED).

223: O Peter, Peter, put up thy sword I prithie heartily
into thy scabbard. / The Gospel of St. John, XVIII,
ii, reads: "Therefore sayd Jesus vnto Peter, Put
vp thy swoorde into the sheath," or "scabbard," as
Douai Version has it (Law, p. 41).

229: Courser / a runner or a racer (OED).

229: Curtall=curtal / a horse with its tail cut short or
docked (and sometimes the ears cropped) (OED).

229: Cut / a common or laboring horse, either from
having the tail cut short or from being cut as a
gelding (Collins).

245: bot / the larva of a botfly; especially one infesting
      the horse (OED).

247: spavin=spuing / a disease of horses that causes
      lameness (OED).

247: splent=spling / a thin piece of wood or other rigid
      material used to hold a fractured or dislocated bone
      in position during the process of reunion (OED).

247: ring-bone / an expstosis on the pastern bones of the
      horse usu. producing lameness (OED).

248: fashion / a corruption of farcin=farcy, from the
      French farcin; a chronicle, ultimately fatal actino-
      mycosis of cattle (Collins; OED).

248: windgall / a soft swelling on the fetlock joint of a
      horse (OED).

248: gall / to fret and sear away by friction; to irritate
      (OED).

249: plaister=plaster / a pasty composition (OED).

251: sheeres=sheep-hair cutter (OED).

253: slouen / to treat slovenly (OED).

260: Imprimis / primarily (CNLD).

260-272: the Ale, the Toast, the Ginger, and the Nutmeg
      ... / One of the fourteen Freemen's sons runs as
      follows:
      "Of all the birds that ever I see,
      The owl is the fairest in her degree;
      For all the day long she sits in a tree,
      And when the night comes, away flies she:
      To whit te whoo! to whom drinkst thou?
      Sir knave, to you.
      This song is well sung I make you a vow,
      And he is a knave that drinketh now:
      Nose, nose, jolly red nose!
      And who gave you that jolly red nose?
      Cinamon, ginger, nutmegs and cloves,
      And that gave me my jolly red nose. "
      Chappell's Popular Music of the Olden Times gives
      the music. This song was printed with a few un-

important variants and omission of the two last
lines in An Antidote against Melancholy: Made up
in Pills, published in 1661 and edited with notes by
J. Woodfall Ebsworth in Choyce Drollery, 1871
(Swaen, p. 404).

266: Galen / a celebrated physician of the second century,
      A. D. , born at Pergamus in Asia Minor (WBD).

267: hart / heart.

271: buffet / a blow; a stroke; now usually one given with
      the hand (OED).

274: precept / command (OED).

286: boord / board, the stage of a theatre; the tablet or
      frame on which some games are played (OED).

[I, iii]

290: a yoong Gentleman, / Thrasibulus.

291: a poore man. / Alcon, Radagon's father.

297: Alate / lately (OED).

297: in a commoditie / "Goods which the prodigal took
      as a part of the sum he wished to borrow from
      the usurer, and which he was to turn into cash
      in the best way he was able" (Dyce, quoted by
      Greg); commodity = goods (Dyce).

298: sirreuerence = salva reverential (M. L.) / saving your
      reverence; with all respect for; with apologies to
      (OED).

310-311: I borrowed of you fortie pounds, etc. / Compare
      the similar trick described in Lodge's Alarum
      against Vsurers (Gosse, ed. , I, 36-37; Collins, I,
      292-293).

319: deuise / a gift of real property by will; a plan (OED).

328: Caterpillar / a rapacious person; an extortionist; one
      who preys upon society (OED).

329: rauening=ravening / greedily searching for prey (OED).

331: recognisance / a bond or obligation of record entered into before court or majestrate, binding a person to do something (OED).

332: sped=speed / to provide or furnish (one) with something (OED).

336: dispatch / to put an end to; to finish quickly (OED).

341: counterpaine=counterpart / the corresponding part of a pair of deeds (Collins).

372: sod milk / =churned milk; sod is the old preterite and past participle of "seethe" (Collins).

375: Prognostication / forecast (OED).

380: churle / peasant; rustic (OED).

394: whilst / until (Dyce).

406: husbandrie / frugality; thrift (OED).

416: rod / a stick; a scepter (OED).

[II, i]

429: despoile / to deprive (OED).

439: Aurora / daughter of Hyperion and Thia (Thea); Goddess of the dawn; (DCM).

445: Mustring=Mustering=Muster / to assemble (OED).

445: Ida / a celebrated mountain in Crete where Zeus was educated. To this mountain Zeus sent Hera, Aphrodite, and Athena for the famous Judgment of Paris (DCM).

448: Myrre=Myrrh / any shrub or tree that yields the gum-resin (OED).

450: Tyre / silk cloth from Tyre in Syria (OED).

454: amisse / faultily; wrongly (OED).

455: tramel=trammel / an instrument (OED).

456: wile / trick, strategem; coquettish trick (OED).

457: coy / to quiet; to soothe; to caress (OED).

457: trick and trim / trickily and smartly designed (OED).

459: smite / to defeat; to beat or dash against (OED).

462: auaile / to be worthy or advantageous (OED).

474: say nay, and take it. / Dyce compares Richard III,
      Act III, Scene vii, 1. 50: "Play the maid's part,
      still answer nay, and take it. " (Collins).

480: rash / reckless, too hasty (OED).

506: Mauors= Mars / a contraction of Mavers or Mavors
      (DCM).

506: Knacks= Eunucks (Greg; Dyce).

513: my penny siluer by her leaue / by his influence he
      would believe anything he says (OED).

515: ward / guard or circle (OED).

515: Magi / the order of Persian priests (OED; DCM).

527: hie / to pant; to gasp for air (OED).

541: Augurer / a Roman fortune teller (DCM).

547: Phoebus / "pure" as an epithet of Apollo, the sun
      god (DCM).

548: Clitia= Clytia= Clytie / daughter of Oceanus and Tethys,
      beloved of Apollo.   She got herself changed into a
      sunflower; thus she is still turning towards sol, one
      of Apollo's names; the symbol of faithfulness, un-
      wavering devotion, and love (DCM).

554: meade / an alcholic liquor made of honey, malt,
      yeast, spice, and water (OED).

555: balmy / fragrant; soft. See 1611.

556: blent / blended (OED); mingled or confounded (Dyce).

556: Hesperus / the evening star, son of Iapetus; brother
      of Atlas; father of Hesperis (DCM; SDM).

557: Scrropes=sirup / Syrup (OED).

558: Balsomo=Balsam / a healthy preservative essence,
      of oil and softly penetrative nature, conceived by
      Paracelsus to exist in all organic bodies (OED).

574: minion / a favorite; a paramour (OED).

574: nonce / occasion (Dyce).

578: meum tuum / What is mine is yours or what is yours
      is mine (CNLD).

579: hence / away (with)!

581: peate=petite (Fr.) / "pet" as an Elizabethan endear-
      ment (Collins).

582: Rasni's adulterous affair with Alvida in the play /
      seems to be parallel with the story of David, King
      of Judah who falls in love with Bathsheba, wife of
      Iriah, the Hittite, although the outcome is not
      identical.

597: craft / skill; dexterity (OED).

598: Marke but the Prophets, etc. / These lines may be
      remedied as
          "Marke but the Prophet, he that shortly showes,
          And after death expects for many, ...woes. "=
      he that points out and expects that woes are at
      hand and will come to many after death (Collins).

[II, ii]

600: the poore man and the Gentleman / See 290 and 291.

604: suffise / to suffice (OED).

610: mease / old form of "mess" (Dyce).

615: dawb- daub / to cover or to paint (OED).

615:    statute lace / formal lace (OED).

615:    mockado / a sort of coarse, or mock velvet (Dyce).

615:    Cape / capeskin (OED).

631:    Runnagate / runnaway (OED).

632:    varlet / rascal; attendant; knave (OED).

634:    ratler / rattlesnake (OED).

643:    Caitife / a mean, evil, or cowardly person (OED).

646:    angel / an English coin with the archangel Michael
        and the Dragon shown on it prior to 1634 (OED).

648:    bullock / a young bull; a castrated bull; an ox (OED).

653:    aduersary / enemy; opponent (OED).

655:    He is not wise, that is not wise for himself. =Non
        sapit qui sibi non sapit. / It is one of the
        commonest proverbs of the Elizabethan writers.
        It is quoted in Lodge's Rosalynde and Nashe's
        P. P. Supplic. to the Devil has "frustra sapit quo
        sibi non..." (In vain he knows who knows not
        himself) (Collins).

655:    He is not wise, etc. / is remindful of "If thou be
        wise, thy wysdome shalt do thy selfe goode" (Pro-
        verbs IX. 12).

660:    plaintife / a complainant; a person who brings a suit
        into a court of law (OED).

669:    equitie / fairness; impartiality; justice (OED).

670:    Signor Mizaldo / the principal character of the Old
        Wives Tale in the Cobbler of Canterbury. He is a
        fellow who has a beautiful wife and is thoroughly
        cajoled by one Peter and his wife (Collins).

682:    redress / compensation (OED).

691:    depose / to state under oath; to testify (OED).

697: brabbing / quarrelling, squabbling (Dyce).

716: tender / to offer in payment of an obligation. (OED).

723: geere=gear / business (Dyce).

726: I hold my cap to a noble / Dyce compares the title-
page of the Second Part of Conny-Catching (1591),
"Which if you reade, without laughing, Ile guiue
you my cap for a noble" (Collins).

752: dubd=dubed / to make one a knight by tapping on the
shoulder with a sword (OED).

767-768: Oseas warns, "Looke so to iudge that at the
latter day, / Ye be not iudge'd with those that
wend astray" / "Iudge not, that ye be not iudged
For with what judgment ye judge, ye shall be
judged:" (Matthew VII. 1-2).

769: passerh / passeth (OED).

[II, iii]

771: Clowne. / the Clowne is undoubtedly Adam in this
scene (Dyce). See 192.

772: Tapster / barmaid; bartender (OED).

798: Paphlagonia / By mistake the quartos make the King
of Paphlagonia enter here (Dyce). He actually
appears in 1. 863.

819: tapt / tapped; to make by tapping (OED).

819: while / until (Dyce).

819: cracke / become harsh (OED).

823: rase / raze (L. radix) (OED).

826: halfcap / strong, heady ale such as makes men set
their caps in a huffing manner (Collins).

838: shitten / disgusting; contemptible (OED).

844: crue=crew (OED).

866:   passing / exceedingly (OED).

874:   blythe=blithe / merry; cheerful; gay (OED).

875:   shift / an entertaining or humorous device (OED).

877:   shroud / to hide; to protect (OED).

878:   arch-ruler / principal-ruler (OED).

881:   battail'd / battle (OED).

884:   querdon / reward; recompense (OED).

892:   broile / to become angry (OED).

901:   vouch=vouchsafe / to deign to accept of something
       (OED).

907:   carouse / a glassful drunk all at once as a toast
       (OED).

924:   obstruction / hindrance (OED).

932:   Sandal / a thin rich silken material (OED).

932:   Sussapine=gassampine (Collins; OED).

934:   Eol=Aolus / God of the winds (DCM).

935:   myrre=myrrh / a fragment, bitter tasting gum resin
       exuded from any of several shrubs of Arabia and
       eastern Africa (OED).

935:   Ambergreece=ambergris / a waxy substance found
       floating in or on the shores of tropical waters,
       used in perfumery as a fixture (OED).

947:   wracke / to destruction; ruin (OED).

[III, i]

951:   Ionas / Jonah in the Old Testament.

953:   steal / to gain artfully (OED).

954:   convey on / to transport; to transmit; to transfer (OED).

954: <u>tone</u> / morale; spirit (<u>OED</u>).

959-961: Ionas's soliloquy, "<u>Loe</u> <u>Israel</u> <u>once</u> <u>that</u> <u>flourisht</u>
        <u>like</u> <u>the</u> <u>vine</u>, / <u>Is</u> <u>barraine</u> <u>laide</u>, <u>the</u> <u>beautiful</u>
        <u>encrease</u> / <u>Is</u> <u>wholly</u> <u>blent</u>, ..." / seems to refer
        to "Israel is an emptie vine, yet hath it brought
        foorth fruite to it selfe, according to the multitude
        of the fruite thereof he hath encreased alwaye"
        (Hosea X. i).

975: <u>Amithais</u> / Bible, King James Version, II, Kings,
     XIV. 25; Jonah, the son of Amittai, the prophet,
     which was of Gath-hepher (<u>DB</u>).

975: <u>Amithais</u> <u>sonne</u>, <u>I</u> <u>charge</u> <u>thee</u> <u>muse</u> <u>no</u> <u>more</u>, /
     "The worde of the Lorde came vnto Jonas the sonne
     of Amittai, saying:" (Jonah I. 1).

978: <u>loines</u>= go girt one's loines / to get ready to do some-
     thing difficult (<u>ODEP</u>).

979: <u>wend</u> / to proceed; to go (<u>OED</u>).

979-981: <u>To</u> <u>Niniuie</u>, <u>that</u> <u>mightie</u> <u>Citie</u> <u>wend</u>, / <u>And</u> <u>say</u>
        <u>this</u> <u>message</u> <u>from</u> <u>the</u> <u>Lord</u> <u>of</u> <u>hoasts</u>, / "Aryse,
        and go to Niniue that great citie, and crye against
        it: for their wickednesse is come vp before me"
        (Jonah I. 2).

981-984: <u>Preach</u> <u>vnto</u> <u>them</u> <u>these</u> <u>tidings</u> <u>from</u> <u>thy</u> <u>God</u>. /
        <u>Behold</u> <u>thy</u> <u>widkednesse</u> <u>hath</u> <u>tempted</u> <u>me</u>, / <u>And</u>
        <u>pierced</u> <u>through</u> <u>the</u> <u>ninefold</u> <u>orbes</u> <u>of</u> <u>heauen</u>. /
        <u>Repent</u>, <u>or</u> <u>else</u> <u>thy</u> <u>iudgement</u> <u>is</u> <u>at</u> <u>hand</u>. / This
        is an interpreted version of the warning of John the
        Baptist, "Repent, for the kingdome of heauen is at
        hande" (Matthew III. 2).

986-1007: Ionas's soliloquy on his refusal to obey God's
        command / "And Ionas rose vp to flee into Tarsis
        from the presence of the Lord" (Jonah I. 3).

986: <u>Prostrate</u> / submissive; lay low (<u>OED</u>).

987: <u>behest</u> / a command; an order (<u>OED</u>).

1005: <u>misgive</u> / to cause fear, doubt, or suspicion in one's mind (OED).

1005-1006, 1041, 1046: And for a while to Tharsus shape
my course, etc. / "And Jonas rose vp to flee into
Tharsis from the presence of the Lord, and went
downe to Joppa, and founde and ship going to Tharsis:
so he payed his fare, and went downe into it, that
he might go with them vnto Tharsis from the presence of the Lord" (Jonah I. 3).

1006 and 1008: Tharsus / Tarshishi (Dyce); Vulgate and
Bishops' Bible, Jonah I. 3, Tharsis; perhaps con-
fused with Tarsus, Acts XI, 25 (Greg). See 1:
Cilicia.

1007: vnfret his angry browes / to clear his forehead of
its frown (OED; Collins).

1010: on / "braue merchants" can not be modified by a
singular numeral, "one." Therefore "come on"
seems more appropriate here.

1014: budget / bag's stock (OED).

1018: cate / delicacy; choice food (OED).

1021: swincke / to move back and forth (OED); to labor,
or to toil (Dyce).

1022: Orious=Orions / a mighty hunter in Greek mythology;
a large and brilliant constellation, figured as a
hunter with a belt and sword (SDM).

1023: load-star / the North Star (OED).

1024: Arcturus / the brightest star in the Constellation. .
Boötes (OED).

1028: stir / steer (Greg).

1032: wot-wit / the first and third persons, singular of
"wit;" to know (OED).

1040: pretend / to intend (Dyce).

1041: Ioppa=Joppa or Joffa / subdistrict, Lydda district,
S. Palestine (WGD).

1041: Tharsus / See 1005-1006.

1041: haven / port; harbor (OED).

1041: here in Ioppa haven / The margin of the Bishops'
       Bible informs us that Ioppa "is an hauen towne in
       the which Peter lodged. " Likewise the Geneva
       Version states that Iapho "was the haven and porte
       to take shipping thither, called also Ioppa" (Law,
       p. 37).

1042: prest / ready; prepared (OED).

1046: hire / the amount paid for getting the services of
       a person or the use of a thing (OED).

1046: Tharsus / See 1005-1006.

1047: budget / See 1014.

1048: To one in peace, / Go on in peace (J. C. Smith
       quoted by Collins).

1049: succoureth / to succor; to help; to relieve (OED).

1053: simony / the buying or selling of sacred or spiritual
       things such as ecclesiastical pardons, church offices,
       etc. (OED).

1054: subtill / subtle (OED).

1058-1059: Oseas's warning, "The axe alreadie to the tree
       is set, / Beware to tempt the Lord ye men of art"
       / seems to be an allusion to Matthew III. 10:
       "Euen now is the axe also put vnto the roote of
       the trees: therefore euery tree which bryngeth not
       foorth good fruite, is hewn downe, and cast into
       fire. " See also Deut. VI, 13.

[III, ii]

1070: flat / plain (OED).

1095-1096: che trow, cha taught him lesson to know his
       father / I believe I taught him ... (Collins);
       Che-Ich-I, a dialect (OED).

1101: qualme / a sudden feeling of uneasiness; scruples; misgiving (OED).

1107: blear / to dim; to blurr; to obscure (OED).

1109: ruthful / full of pity or sorrow (OED).

1111: guile / cunning; deceitful conduct (OED).

1113: plundge=plunge / a drive or downward leap; difficulty (OED); straits, distress (Dyce).

1117: callet=calletta / Callet or callat, a strumpet or scold (OED).

1123: pap / a woman's breast; soft-food for infants (OED).

1128: furrowes / deep tracks (OED).

1138: Titus=Tityus / giant son of Jupiter. He was cast into the innermost hell for insulting Diana (SDM).

1142: bane / See 34.

1144: vntoward / stubborn; unruly (OED).

1144: peruerse / perverted; wicked (OED).

1169: mickle / much (OED).

1170: towardnesse / docileness; favorableness (OED).

1184: sooth / truth (OED).

1208: caitive / See 643.

1210: scurruie / hasty (OED).

1210: trull / See 79.

1211: lump / a dull person (OED).

1212: Lossell=Losel / a worthless person, a rake; a scoundrel (OED).

1216: Arsmetry=a corruption of Arsmetrick / arithmetic by form association with geometry (Collins).

1216: Additiori multiplicarum / multiplied additions (CNLD).

1236: repine / to complain; to fret with (OED).

1238: rupture / a breaking off of friendly relations (OED).

1244: Satrapos= satrapes / the governor of a province in
       ancient Persia; a ruler of a dependency, often a
       despotic, subordinate official; a petty tyrant (OED).

1247: Potentate / ruler; monarch (OED).

1252: spue / to spew; to vomit (OED).

1253: Vulueus= Vulcans (Greg); the Roman name for the
       God of fire and metal working (DCM).

1260: studde= stud / a metal crossbar bracing a link; a
       stem or trunk (OED).

1292: Radagon's ingratitude toward his starving parents
       and younger brother is described as "The swoord
       of iustice drawne alreadie is. " / this is an echo
       of "The sworde is drawne" (Ezekiel XXI. 29).

[III, iii]

1293: the Clowne / He is Adam in this scene. See 192.

1299: ostry fagot= hostry faggot / a faggot in a hostlery
       (Dyce); a fire laid in an inn, when one is set alight,
       the guests take care to keep it alight (Collins).

1308: borachio= Sp. borracha / a leathern bag or bottle
       for wine (Collins).

1328: beswindge= beswinge/ to hand (OED).

1329: proffer / to offer (OED).

1339: white son / "white" is an epithet of endearment
       (Dyce).

1347: brue / brow, brew, variations of "broo"; liquor,
       juice to brew (OED).

1347: bake / to be infuriated (Dyce).

1356:   Lease parol= Lease, parol / Lease per Parol; a
        lease by word of mouth (Collins).

1361-1362: Oseas's prophesey, "For if the feete the head
        shall hold in scorne, / The Cities state will fall
        and be forlorne" / seems to refer to "And the eye
        can not say vnto the hande, I haue no neede of
        thee: Nor, the head agayne to the feete, I haue no
        neede of you" (I Corinthians XII. 21).

1366-1367: "Let loue abound, and vertue raigne in all, /
        So God will hold his hand that threateneth thrall" /
        seem to echoe the idea, "Let brotherly loue continue"
        (Hebrews XIII, 1).

[IV, i]

1368:   Tharsus / See 1006 and 1008.

1378-1430: The ship master describes the storm in detail.
        / This seems Lodge's dramatization of the Biblical
        reference in Jonah I. 4: "But the Lorde sent out a
        great winde into the sea, and there was a mightie
        tempest in the sea, so that the shippe was in daunger
        of splitting in sunder. "

1378:   Trion / a name for the seven principal stars in
        Ursa Major, also called Charles's Wain (OED).
        See 1379: Bootes' Wain.

1379:   Bootes' Wain / Boote is a northern constellation,
        the wagoner, situated in the tail of the Great Bear
        and containing the bright star Arcturus (OED). Wain
        is the group of seven bright stars in the constellation
        called the Great Bear: more fully Charles's Wain
        (OED).

1382:   blithful / cheerful (OED).

1383:   aramine / hastily; vigorously (OED).

1385:   sable / black (OED).

1386-1388: Gan to eclips Lucinas siluer face, etc. / "But
        the Lorde sent out a great winde into the sea, and
        there was a mightie tempest in the sea, for that the
        shippe was in daunger of splitting in sunder" (Jonah

I. 4).

1386: Lucina / daughter of Jupiter and Juno. The Roman
goddess of the travails of women and of childbirth
(DCM; SDM).

1387: hurling / rushing violently (OED; Collins).

1388: billow / a large wave; great swell of water (OED).

1389: scantle / to shorten (OED).

1390: drabler / an additional piece of canvas, laced to
the bottom of the bonnet of a sail, to give it greater
depth (Collins).

1392: trusse / to tie; to fasten (OED).

1397: welny=well-night / almost (OED).

1401: Bisas=Bise's / of the north wind (Greg).

1402: rudeer / middle (Greg).

1403-1406: 1408-1410: There might you see with pale and
gastly lookes, etc. / "Then the maryners were
afraide, and cryed euery man vnto his God, and
cast the wares that were in the shippe into the sea,
to lighten it of them: but Jonas was gone downe into
the sides of the shippe, and he laye downe sleeping"
(Jonah I. 5).

1407: swage / to bend; to swing (OED).

1408-1410: See 1403-1406.

1410: succour / help; relief (OED).

1411-1415: Him I awooke, and said why slumberest thou?
etc. / "And the shippe maister to him, and said
What meanest thou sleeper? Vp and cast vpon thy
God, if to be that God wyl shine vnto vs, that we
perishe not" (Jonah I. 6).

1414: amisse / astray (OED).

1414-1416: Then cast we lots to know by whose amisse,

etc. / "And they saide euery one to his felow,
Come, let vs cast lottes; that we may know for
whose cause this euil is on vs. And they cast
lottes: and the lotte fel on Jonas" (Jonah I. 7).

1418:   Then questioned we his country and his name, etc.
/ "Then said they vnto him: Tell vs for whose
cause is this euill come vpon vs? What is thyne
occupation? Whence camest thou? What countrey
man art thou; and of what nation?" (Jonah I. 8).

1419-1421:   Who answered vs, I am an Hebrue borne, etc.
/ "And he answered them: I am an Hebrue, and I
fear the Lorde God of heauen, which hath made the
sea, and the drye lande (Jonah I. 9); Then were
the men exceedingly afraide, and saide vnto him:
Why hast thou done this? (for the men knewe that
he fled from the presence of the Lorde, because
he had tolde them)" (Jonah I. 10).

1423:   carkasse / the body (OED).

1423-1424:   Take me and cast my carkasse in the sea,
etc. / "And he saide vnto them, Take me, and cast
me into the sea, and the sea shalbe calme vnto
you: for I know that for my sake this great tempest
is vpon you" (Jonah I. 12).

1427:   But when no Oares nor labour might suffice, etc. /
"Neuertheless, the men assayed with rowing to bring
the shippe to lande, but they could not, because the
sea wrought, and was troublous against them"
(Jonah I. 13).

1428-1429:   We heaued the haplesse Ionas ouer-boord. etc.
/ "So they toke vp Jonas, and cast him into the sea,
and the sea left raging" (Jonah I. 15).

1439:   Gossampine / Gassampine for gossampine cotton
cloth, a kind of cloth made of the cotton-like fibre
(OED).

1440:   addict / to give assent (OED).

1441-1442:   Then suffer vs most mightie Gouernour, etc. /
"And the men feared the Lorde exceedingly, and
offered a sacrifice vnto the Lorde, and made vowes"

(Jonah I. 16).

1446: Ethnicks / heathens (OED).

1446-1459: Oseas's soliloquy on God's wrath / corresponds
"And they saide vnto him; what shal we do vnto thee,
that the sea may be calme vnto us: for the sea
wrought, and was troublous, / And he saide vnto
them, Take me, and cast me into the sea, and the
sea shalbe calme vnto you: for I know that for my
sake this great tempest is vpon you" (Jonah I. 11-
12).

1455: Oseas's assertion, "The Lord is just" / reflects
Isaiah XLV. 19: "I am the Lorde, whiche when I
speake, do declare the thing that is righteous and
true. "

1455: slime / any moist or sticky substance that is
considered filthy (OED).

[IV, ii]

1460-1461: Ionas the Prophet is cast out of the Whales
belly vpon the Stage. / "And the Lorde spake vnto
the fifthe, and it cast out Ionas vpon the drye lande"
(Jonah II. 10).

1462-1465: Lord of the light, thou maker of the world,
etc. / "And Jonas prayed vnto the Lorde his God
out of the fisshes belly" (Jonah II. 1).

1467: Leuiathan= Leviathan / a sea monster; a whale
(OED;. DB, pp. 505-506).

1470: scaly / mean; despicable (OED).

1471: chappes= chaps / chops; jaws (OED).

1471: humble stress / stretch, or simple stretch (OED).

1471: tresse / straining (Greg).

1477-1485: I trouble Lord I called vnto thee, etc. / "And
saide: In affliction I cryed vnto the Lorde, and he
heard me: out of the belly of hell cryed I, and thou
heardest my voyce. Thou hadst cast me downe into

the deepe, into the middest of the sea, and the
floods compassed me about: all the billowes and
waues passed ouer me.   And I said, I am cast
away out of thy sight... The weedes were wrapt
about my head.   I went downe to the bottome of
the mountaines, ... yet has ye brought vp my life
from corruption, O Lord my God" (Jonah II. 2-6).

1486-1487:   On thee I thought when as my soule did faint,
etc. / "When my soule fainted within me, I re-
membered the Lorde, and my prayer came in vnto
thee into thy holy temple" (Jonah II. 7).

1487:   prease / to press (Dyce).

1488-1489:   My praiers did prease before thy mercy seate.
etc. / "But I wyll sacrifice vnto thee with the voyce
of thankesgeuing, and wyll pay that that I haue vowed:
for saluation is of the Lorde" (Jonah II. 9).

1489:   For why / Because (Dyce).   See 89.

1491-1492:   The Angell appeareth. etc. / "And the worde
of the Lord came vnto Jonas the second time, saying: Aryse, and go to Niniue that great citie, and
preache against it the preaching which I speake vnto
thee" (Jonah III. 1-2).

1498:   Niniuie / In the scene the seashore near Nineveh
is represented.   Nineveh was, however, an inland
town, not nearer than two hundred miles to the sea
and, according to the Biblical account, three days'
journey from the place where Jonah received the
second command from the Lord (Jonah III. 3).

1499:   towres / See "Six hundreth Towers that toplesse
touch the cloudes" (19).

1507-1508:   Oseas's brief mention at the end of the scene,
"Who knowes his maisters will and doth it not,
etc. " / is an allusion to "And the seruant, that
knewe his maisters wyll, and prepared not hym
selfe, neither dyd accordyng to his wyll, and shalbe
beaten with many strypes" (Luke XII. 47).

1551:   passing / exceedingly (OED).

1561:   Pheere=fere, feere, pheare, or pheer / a companion
        or associate (Collins; OED; Dyce).

1571:   beshrow / to curse (OED).

1581:   axier / for "axis"; axletree (Greg).

1586:   droupe=droop / to become weakened (OED).

1592:   Jove=Jupiter / chief of the gods of the ancients.
        A Roman name for Zeus (DCM).

1592:   Juno=Hera / daughter of Cronus and Rhea; sister
        and wife of Zeus; goddess of women and of child-
        birth. Also queen of the gods and of heaven. The
        most jealous wife in mythology (DCM).

1594:   sutes Speori / suits his pennons (Greg).

1596:   Galbocia / Galatea (Dyce); a daughter of Nerues and
        Doris; a statue of a maiden carved in ivory by
        Pygmalion, King of Cyprus; he fell in love with it
        and it was given life by Aphrodite (DCM).

1600:   Onoris=Orions / famous giant, blinded by Oenopion
        for grievous wrong done to Merope; he was exiled
        from Chios (SDM).

1601:   enchast=enchase / to ornament by engraving; to
        engrave (OED).

1601:   carbunckle / any of certain deep-red gems, espe-
        cially a garnet with a smooth, convex surface (OED).

1605:   Lucina / See 1386.

1606:   Medusa / one of the three Gorgons, daughter of
        Phorcys and Ceto. She was noted for her charms
        and beauty of her hair, which Minerva changed into
        serpents (SDM).

1610:   blend / to disturb or to break (Greg).

1611:   balme /any fragrant ointment or aromatic oil for

healing or anointing.   See 555.

1612:   closure / finish (OED).

1614:   Morne=morn / the dawn; sunrise (Greg).

1614:   Cephalus / married Procris, whom he accidentally
        killed by shooting while she was secretly watching
        him; he though she was a wild beast.   Cephalus
        was the type of constancy, too (SDM).

1616:   Caitiff / the cowardly (OED).

1622:   adyts=additte= Latin adyta / the innermost secret
        part of sanctuary of a temple; inner shrine (OED).

1625:   Ve=Vae / woe!; alas! (CNLD).

1633:   Morpheus / son of Sleep, and the god of dreams;
        the God of Sleep (DCM).

1638:   brandish / to flourish; to shake menacingly; to wave
        (OED).

1641:   clammy / cold or moist (OED).

1642:   retrograde / contrary; moving backward (OED).

1646:   betoken / to foreshadow; to indicate (OED).

1648:   potentate / a ruler; a monarch (OED).

1658:   Oseas's reference to "...pride will haue a fall"
        / appears to be an echo of Solomon's words, "Pryde
        goeth before destruction, and an hygh minde before
        the fall" (Proverbs XVI. 18).

1661-1662:   Oseas's assertion, "Who byild one fate, and
        leaue the corner stone, / The God of Gods, sweete
        Christ the onely one" / seems to be an allusion to
        "And are built vpon the foundation of the apostles
        and prophetes, Jesus Christe hym selfe beying the
        head corner stone" (Ephesians II. 20).

[IV, iv]

1693:   Tong / the vibrating end of the reed in a wind

instrument (OED).

1695:   Spritus santus=spiritus sanctus / Holy Spirit or
         Holy Ghost (CNLD).

1698:   Nominus patrus=Nominus patris / Father's name
         (CNLD).

1701:   Ale / ale-house (Collins); a festival where much
         ale was drunk: hence bride-ale, church-ale, clerk-
         ale, etc. (Dyce).

1725:   cudgell=cudgel / a short thick stick used as a
         weapon; a club (OED).

1734:   tall / bold, brave (Dyce).

[IV, v]

1740:   prie=to pry / to spy; to look closely or curiously
         (OED).

1741:   pilfer / to plunder (OED).

1744:   broaking=broking / money-lending (OED).

1745:   ware / anything made to sell (OED).

1747:   posie / a verse or motto inscribed inside a ring
         (OED).

1747-1748: a horn thumb / an instrument used by pick-
         pockets in the form of a case or thimble of horn
         put on the thumb to resist the edge of their knife
         in the act of cutting purses (Collins).

1760:   crust / a man of audacity or insolence (OED).

1763:   Ecce signum / Behold; look at the sign (CNLD).

1764:   pilferer / a stealer (OED).

1773:   smocke / a chemise (OED).

1775:   trill-lill=trillil / to drink with a trilling sound
         (OED).

1794-1796: Jonas's warning, "Yet but fortie daies remaining,
etc. " / represents the idea of Jonah III. 4: "And
Jonas began to enter into the citie a dayes iourney,
and he cryed and saide: yet fourtie dayes, and
Niniuie shaltbe destroyed. "

1797-1800: The repentance scene / is a dramatization of
Jonah III, 5: And the men of Niniuie beleued God,
and proclamed a fast, and put on sackecloth from
the greatest of them to the leafste of them. "

1816: prankt / to adorn (OED).

1817: powle / to poll or to plunder (Greg).

1827: hainous=heinous / hateful; wicked (OED).

1834: Jonas's description of God, "For God is iust as he
is merciful" / refers to the same idea expressed in
Deuteronomy XXXII. 4 and Isaiah XLV. 21.

⌈V, i]

1851: Borachious=Sp. borracha / See 1308.

1852: blythsome=blithesome / lighthearted (OED).   See 874.

1859: brightsome / lively; illustrous (OED).

1860: skinck=M. E. schenchen / to pour out liquor (Collins);
to fill, properly pour (Greg); to draw, pour out, or
serve liquor (Dyce).

1861: carouse / hilarious drinking party (OED).

1871, 1873: Crete / The King of Crete in I, i (129-134)
is dismissed, but reappears here and in 1873 without explanation.   Greg dismisses it as a result of
collaboration (Greg).

1915: port royal / port rivel, a landing place, or a river
port (Greg).

1922: Juniper / Gin (OED).

1945: ruffle / to swagger; to brawl (OED).

1947: cholloricke=choleric / quick tempered (OED).

1948: fustian / pompous or bombastic (OED).

1956: standerd-standard / standardbearer (OED).

1957: ply / to yield (OED).

1959: tane=to tone / to become lowered, weakened (Scot-
       tish and Northern dialect) (OED).

1981: indenture / a written contract (OED).

1991: Ionas's reference to Rasni, "Your King loues
       chambering and wantonnesse" / seems to represent
       "Let vs walke honestly as in the day, not in riotyng
       and drunkenesse, neither in chaunmberying and
       wantonnesse, neither in strife and envying" (Romans
       XIII. 13).

1992: distaine / to dishonor (OED).

1994-1995: Ionas's warning, "Behold therefore all like a
       strumpet foule, etc. / is an allusion to Ezekiel
       XVI. 38: "Moreouer I wyll iudge thee as a breaker
       of wedlocke and a murtherer, and recompence thee
       thyne owne blood in wrath and gelousie."

1996: Another warning, "The foe shall pierce the gates
       with iron rampes" / is an allusion to Ezekiel XXI.
       22: "... to set battle rammes agaynst the gates,
       to cast a vulwarke, and to builde a fort."

1996: rampe / a sloping passage (OED).

1997: Ionas's further warning, "The fire shall quite con-
       sume thee, etc." / refers to II Kings I. 10: "If I
       be a man of God, let fyre come downe from heauen
       and consume thee and thy fiftie."

2000-2001: Lamana; Thine eldest sister is Lamana. /
       And Sodome on thy right hand seated is. / Dyce
       regards Lamana as a corruption; Grosart proposes
       Gomorrah; Deighton, El Adama; J. C. Smith, Samaria.
       Furthermore, Collins pronounces Samaria as an
       "almost certain conjecture," and cites several pass-
       ages from Hosea and Ezekiel in proof. However,

there is the wording of Ezekiel, XVI, 46 in the Bishops' Bible: "Thine eldest sister is Samaria, she and her daughters that dwel / vpon thy left hand, but thy younger sister, that dwelleth on thy right hand, is Sodoma and her daughters" (Law, p. 40).

2018-2020: Lords see proclaim'd, yea see it straight proclaim'd, etc. / "And he caused a cryer to crye, and say through the citie by the counsell of the King and his nobles, Let me neither man nor beast, bullocke nor sheepe, taste ought at all, neigher feede, nor drinke water" (Jonah III. 7).

2021: Perhaps the Lord will yeeld and pittie vs. / "Who can tel whether God wyl turne and be moued with repentaunce, and turne from his fierce wrath, that we perishe not?" (Jonah III. 9).

2022: Bear hence these wretched blandishments of sinne, / "And let both man and beast put on sackcloth, and crye mightyly vnto God: yea let euery man turne from his euill way, and from the wickednesse that is in his handes" (Jonah III. 8).

2022: blandishment / flattery (OED).

2023: And bring me sackcloth to attire your King. / "And worde came vnto the King of Niniue: Which arose from his throne, and put of his robe, and coured him selfe with sackcloth, and sate downe in ashes" (Jonah III. 6).

2026: a man / an attendant, to execute Rasni's orders (Dyce).

[V, ii]

2043: groning= groan / to suffer deeply from cruelty; to be loaded weigh down (OED).

2046-2047: The Usurer's expression about the stumbling-block, "Tread where I lift, mee-thinkes the bleeding ghostes, / Of those.. etc. / refers to Leviticus XIX. 14 and Ezekiel III. 20.

2055: The Usurer's words, "Your mountaines shroude me

from the God of truth" / echoes the words of St.
John: "And sayde to the hylles and rockes, fall on
ve, and hyde vs from the presence of hun ⌈sic⌉ that
sitteth on the throne, and from the wrath of the
lamb" (Revelation VI. 16).

2057:   The Usurer's fear, "See how he blots me out of
        the booke of life" / refers to Psalm LXIX. 27:
        "Let them be wyped out of the booke of the livyng"
        and to Revelation II. 5: "and I wyll not put out his
        name out of the booke of life."

2058:   Aetna / a volcanic mountain in the N. E. of Sicily.
        Zeus buried under it Typhon or Encedadus (ECM).

2060:   Licas-Lycus / See 13.

2063:   reprobate / depraved; unsaved (OED).

2074:   stale / corruption (OED).

2077:   rigor / harshness; strickness (OED).

2081:   broydred-broider / to embroider (OED).

2086:   mortifie / to punish (OED).

2086:   pamper / to feed too much (OED).

2101:   No Lord enters until 2104. So the Lords are not
        speaking at this time.

2124:   Aeolus / See 67.

2127:   The King of Cilicia's advice to Fasni, "Heauens are
        prepitious vnto faithful priers" / represents Solomon's
        words, "The Lorde is farre from the vngodly: but
        he heareth the prayer of the ryghteous" (Proverbs
        XV. 29) and "The feruent prayer of a ryghteous
        man auaileth much" (James V. 16).

2127:   propitious / gracious; favorable (OED).

⌈V, iii⌉

2158:   Assur / Assyria (WGD).

2171-2174: Here will I sit me downe and fixe mine eye,
etc. / "And Jonas went out of the citie, and sate
him downe on the east side thereof, and there made
him a boothe, and sate vnder it in the shadowe, till
he might see what should be downe in the citie"
(Jonah IV. 5).

2173-2174: And lo a pleasant shade, a spreading vine, etc.
/ "And the Lord God prepared a gourd, and made
it spring vp ouer Jonas, that it might be a shadowe
ouer his head, to deliuer him from his great griefe:
So Jonas was exceeding glad to the gourde" (Jonah
IV. 6).

2175-2177: What meanes my God, the day is done and
spent, etc. / "And this displeased Jonas greatly,
and he was angrye [within himselfe"] (Jonah IV. 1).

2177: wroth=wrath / angry; wrathful (OED).

2178-2184: I pray thee Lord remember what I said, etc.
"And he prayed vnto the Lorde, and saide: I pray
thee O Lorde, was not this my saying when I was
yet in my countrey? therefore I hasted to flee into
Tharsis: For I knewe that thou art a gratious God,
and mercifull, long suffering, and of great kindnesse,
and repentest thee of euill" (Jonah IV. 2).

2183: sufferance / suffering; patient endurance (OED).

2183: Full of compassion and of sufferance, / Bishops'
Bible, IV. 2: "Merciful, long suffering"; Geneva
Bible: "Merciful, slow to anger" (Law, p. 36).

2185: Why staies thy hand? O Lord first take my life, /
"And nowe O Lorde, take I beseche thee my lyfe
from me: for it is better for me to dye, then to
lyue" (Jonah IV. 3).

2187-2190: Ah he is wroth, behold the gladsome vine, etc.
"But God prepared a worme, when the morning rose
the next day, which smote the gourde, that it withered" (Jonah IV. 7).

2191-2201: Now furious Phlegon triumphs on my browes,
etc. / "And when the sunne rose, God prepared a
feruent east Winde, and the sunne beat vpon the head

of Jonas that he fainted: and withed vnto her soule, that he might dye, and saide, it is better for me to dye, then to lyue" (Jonah IV. 8).

2194: Art thou so angry Jonas? tell me why? / "Then said the Lord, Doest thou wel to be angry?" (Jonah IV. 4).

2195: plungde / overwhelmed (Greg); distressed, driven to straits (Dyce).

2199: Caricular / of the dog-star days (OED).

2202-2203: Ionas art thou so angry for the vine? etc. / "Then saide the Lorde, Thou hast had compassion on the gourde about the Wind thou bestowedst no labour, neither madest it growe: Which cam vp in a night, and perished in a night:" (Jonah IV. 10).

2205: On which thou never labor didst bestow, / Bishops' Bible, Ionas IV. 10: "About the which thou bestowedst no labour"; Geneva Version, "For the which thou hadst not laboured" (Law, p. 36).

2207: dide / died (Greg).

2208-2212: And should not I haue great compassion, etc. "And shall not I spare Niniue that great citie. in the which are more then sixscore thousand persons that knowe not their right hand and their left, and also much cattaile?" (Jonah IV. 11).

2214: contrition / earnest repentance (OED).

2216-2217: Then from the Lord proclaime a mercie day, etc. / "And God sawe their workes, that they turned from their euil wayes, and he repented of the euill that he saide he woulde do vnto them, and did it not" (Jonah III. 10).

2232: rauisht / to overjoy (OED).

2232: spright / brisk; liveliness; gayousness (OED).

2238: slop / slops were wide breeches, trousers (Dyce).

[V, iv]

2241:   lent=Lent / the period including 40 weekdays extend-
        ing from Ash Wednesday to Easter-eve, observed
        as a time of fasting and penitence, in commemo-
        ration of our Lord's fasting in wilderness (DB).

2241:   read-herings cob / a small young red herring (OED);
        the young of a red-herring. Herring-cob was a
        scant term for a herring in general. Cob is from
        the Saxon cop, the head: Gifford observes that old
        writers commonly use it in compound words as a
        distinctive mark of bulk (Dyce).

2243:   I could award with / I could endure (Dyce).

2249:   buttry=buttery / a place for storing liquor (OED).

2250:   ecce signum! / See 1763.

2251:   manchet / a fine white bread (Collins).

2257:   victuals / food and other provisions (OED).

2267:   oryson=orison / prayer (OED).

2283:   where / whereas (Dyce).

2286:   modicum non nocet ut medicus daret / a little bit
        (of medicine) does not hurt as the doctor will give
        it (CNLD).

2295:   untrusse / to undress or to undo (OED).

2300:   marry / an exclamation of surprise or anger (OED).

2306:   while / until (Dyce).

2307:   perforce / necessarily (OED).

[V, v]

2316:   Imence / Incense (Greg).

2323-2326: Ionas warns Alvida against further trans-
        gression: "Let not the nicenesse of your beautious
        lookes, etc." / represents the idea expressed in

Ezekiel XXI. 26: "Thus saith the Lorde God, I
wyll take away the Diademe, and put of the crowne:
this shalbe no more the same, I wyll the humble,
and abase hun ⌈sic.⌉ that is hye. "

2330: whilome=while / at times; once upon a time (OED).

2337: salue / to soothe; to assuage (OED).

2339: behest / a command; an order (OED). See 987.

2347: sheaues=sheave / a wheel with a grooved rim (OED).

2348-2352: Ionas reassures Alvida, saying, "Blest may
you be, like to the flouring sheaues, etc. " /
is an allusion to Luke XV. 7: "I say vnto you,
that lykewyse ioy shalbe in heaun ouer one sinner
that repenteth, more then ouer ninetie and nine
iust persons, which neede no repentaunce. "

2349-2350: Ionas hails the legitimate betrothal of King
Rasni to Alvida in the words: Like Oliue branches
let your children spred: / And as the pines in
loftie Libanon, / Compare the Bishops' Bible, Osea,
XIV. 6: "His branches shall spreade out abroade
and be as fayre as / the olive tree; and swelle as
Libanus" (Law, p. 40).

2351: Lepher / Dyce suggests "Sepher," which the Vulgate gives in Numbers XXXIII, 23-24 for the Shapher
of our authorized version (Quoted in Collins).

2362: purloynd=purlin / a piece of timber laid horizontally
to support the common rafters of a roof (OED).

2363: proffer / See 1329.

2364: owe / own (Dyce).

2384: Actean / coastal; Attic (Greg).

2385: dandle / to dance up and down on the knee or in
the arm (OED).

2394: impudence / indiscreet speech or behavior (OED).

2398: larum=alarm / warning (OED).

2407: <u>Romish</u> / a Roman Catholic (<u>OED</u>).

2408: <u>overshead</u> / to overshadow (<u>OED</u>).

V. Bibliography

Arber, Edward, ed. A Transcript of the Stationers'
  Registers. 2 vols. London: Privately printed,
  1875-1894.

Baskerville, Charles R. "A Prompt Copy of A Looking
  Glass for London and England." Modern Philology,
  XXX (1932), 29-51.

Bowers, Fredson. Principles of Bibliographical Description. New York: Russell and Russell, 1962.

Bradbrook, M. C. The Growth and Structure of Elizabethan
  Comedy. Baltimore: Penguin Books, 1963.

Brown, J. M. "An Early Rival of Shakespeare." New
  Zealand Magazine, II (1877), 119-133.

Burrage, Henry S., ed. Early English and French Voyages
  Chiefly from Hakluyt 1534-1608.

Carl, Richard Ernst. Uber Thomas Lodges Leben und
  Werke. Hall A. S.: Druck von Ehrardt Karras,
  1887.

Cassell's New Latin Dictionary, ed. R. V. Marchant and
  Joseph F. Charles. New York: Funk and Wagnall's
  1965.

Chambers, E. K. The Elizabethan Stage. 4 vols. Oxford:
  Clarendon Press, 1961.

Clugston, George Alan. "A Looking Glasse for London
  and England by Thomas Lodge and Robert Greene,
  A Critical Edition," Unpublished Ph. D. dissertation,
  University of Michigan, 1967.

Collier, John Payne, ed. Extracts from the Registers of
  the Stationers' Company of Works Entered for
  Publication Between the Years 1557 and 1570.

London: Shakespeare Society, 1848 and 1849 [Nos. 38 and 41].

Collins, J. Churton, ed. The Plays and Poems of Robert Greene. 2 vols. Oxford: Clarendon Press, 1905.

Columbia Encyclopedia, ed. William Bridgwater and Seymour Kurtz. New York: Columbia University Press, 1961.

Cotham, Margaret Mary. "Greene and Lodge's A Looking Glass for London and England." Thesis, University of Texas, August, 1928.

Deighton, Kenneth. The Old Dramatists Conjectural Readings on the Texts of Marston, Beaumont and Fletcher, Peele, Marlowe, Chapman, Heywood, Greene, Middleton, Dekker, Webster. Westminster: Archibald Constable, 1896.

Dickinson, Thomas H., ed. The Complete Plays of Robert Greene. London: F. F. Unwin, 1909.

Dictionary of Classical Mythology, ed. J. E. Zimmerman. New York: Harper and Row, 1964.

Dictionary of Latin Literature, ed. James H. Mantinband. New York: Philosophical Library, 1956.

Dictionary of the Bible, ed. James Hastings. 5 vols. New York: Scribner's, 1898-1904.

Downer, Alan S. The British Drama: A Handbook and Brief Chronicle. New York: Appleton-Century-Crofts, 1963.

Dyce, Alexander, ed. The Dramatic and Poetical Works of Robert Greene. 2 vols. London: William Pickering, 1831.

_____, ed. The Dramatic and Poetical Works of Robert Greene and George Peele. London: Routledge, 1861.

Encyclopedic Dictionary of the Bible, ed. Adrianus van den Born; trans. Louis F. Hartman. New York: McGraw-Hill, 1963.

The Encyclopedia of Classical Mythology, ed. Andreas R.
    A. van Aken. Englewood Cliffs, N. J.: Prentice
    Hall, 1965.

Farmer, John S., ed. A Looking Glasse for London and
    England, Tudor Facsmile Texts. Amersham, 1914.

Fleay, Frederick G. A Chronicle History of the Life and
    Work of William Shakespeare, Player, Poet, and
    Playmaker. New York: Scribner and Welford,
    1886.

_____. A Biographical Chronicle of the
    English Drama 1559-1642. 2 vols. London: Reeves
    and Turner, 1891.

Ford, Boris, ed. The Age of Shakespeare. Baltimore:
    Penguin Books, 1962.

Gayley, Charles Mills, Representative English Comedies:
    from the Beginnings to Shakespeare. 2 vols. New
    York: Macmillan, 1930.

Gosse, Edmund W. ed. The Complete Works of Thomas
    Lodge. New York: Russell and Russell, 1963.
    [Reprint of the Hunterian Club ed.].

Gosse, Edmund W. Seventeenth Century Studies. London:
    William Henemann, 1914.

Gosson, Stephen. The School of Abuse, ed. Edward Arber.
    London: Alex. Murray, 1869.

Greenslade, S. L. , ed. Cambridge History of the Bible:
    The West from the Reformation to the Present Day.
    Cambridge: University Press, 1963.

Greg, W. W. A Bibliography of the English Printed Drama
    to the Restoration. 4 vols. London: Bibliographi-
    cal Society, 1939. [Vol. I: Stationers' Records:
    Plays to 1616: Nos. 1-349].

_____. , ed. Henslowe's Diary. 3 vols.
    London: A. H. Bullen, 1904-1908.

_____. , ed. Lodge's Rosalynde Being the
    Original of Shakespeare's As You Like It. New York:

Duffield, 1907.

_____. , ed. A Looking-Glasse for London
and England By Thomas Lodge and Robert Greene,
1594. London: Malone Society, 1932.

_____. , "A Review of J. C. Collins's The
Plays and Poems of Robert Greene. " Modern
Language Review, I (1906), 238-251.

Grosart, Alexander B. , ed. The Life and Complete Works
in Prose and Verse of Robert Greene. 15 vols.
London: Privately printed, 1881-1883.

Grubb, Marion. "Lodge's Borrowing from Ronsard. "
Modern Language Notes, XLV (1930), 357-359.

Hall, Vernon, Jr. Renaissance Literary Criticism: A
Study of Its Social Content. Gloucester, Mass. :
Peter Smith, 1959.

Halliday, F. E. A Shakespeare Companion, 1550-1950.
London: Gerald Duckworth, 1952.

Harrison, G. B. Elizabethan Plays and Players. Ann
Arbor: University of Michigan Press, 1961.

Harrison, O. B. , Jr. English Literary Criticism: The
Renaissance. New York: Appleton-Century-Crofts,
1963.

Harper's Topical Concordance, comp. Charles R. Joy.
New York: Harper, 1962.

The Holy Bible [King James Version]. Cleveland: World
Publishing Company, 1954.

The Interpreter's Dictionary of the Bible, ed. George A.
Buttrick, et al. 4 vols. New York: Abingdon Press,
1962.
Jordan, John Clark. Robert Greene. Columbia University
Press, 1915.

Josephus, Flavius. The Great Roman-Jewish War: A. D.
66-70, trans. William Whiston; rev. D. S. Margo-
liouth; ed. William R. Farmer. New York: Harper,
1960.

_____. Works. 3 vols., trans. William
Whiston. New York: A. L. Burt, [n. d.].

Judges, A. V. , ed. The Elizabethan Underworld. New
York: Dutton, 1930.

Knappen, M. M. Tudor Puritanism: A Chapter in the
History of Idealism. Chicago: University of
Chicago Press, 1965.

Law, Robert Adger. "A Looking Glasse and the Scriptures. " University of Texas Studies (1930), pp.
31-47.

_____. "Two Parellels to Greene and
Lodge's Looking-Glass. " Modern Language Notes,
XXVI (1911), 146-148.

Mackenzie, W. Roy. The English Moralities from the
Point of View of Allegory. New York: Gordian
Press, 1966.

McKerrow, Ronald B. , ed. A Dictionary of Printers and
Booksellers in England, Scotland and Ireland, and
of Foreign Printers of English Books, 1557-1640.
London: Bibliographical Society, 1910.
_____. An Introduction to Bibliography
for Literary Students. Oxford: Clarendon Press,
1965.

_____. Printers' and Publishers'
Devices in England and Scotland 1485-1640. London:
Bibliographical Society, 1949.

McMillan, Mary Evelyn. "An Edition of Greenes Vision
and A Maidens Dreame by Robert Greene. " Diss. ,
University of Alabama, 1960.

McNeir, Waldo F. "The Date of A Looking Glasse for
London. " Notes & Queries, CC (1955), 282-283.

Microfilms [Quartos in microfilms]:

A (1594). Huntington Library copy. STC 16679,
Reel 336.

B (1598). Huntington Library copy. STC 16680,

Reel 406.

C (1602). British Museum copy.   STC 16681, Reel
810.

D (1617). Huntington Library copy.   STC; 16682,
Reel 810.

Ann Arbor, Michigan: University Microfilms.

Microfilms [Bibles in microfilms]:

The Bishops' Bible.   Huntington Library copy.
STC 2099, Reel 1020.

The Geneva Bible.   Huntington Library copy.
STC 2095, Reel 1019.

Ann Arbor, Michigan: University Microfilms.

Microprint [Quarto in microprint]:

A (1594).   New York: Readex Microprint, 1960
[Three Centuries of Drama Series, No. 126].

Nelson's Complete Concordance of the Revised Standard
    Version Bible.   comp. John W. Ellison.   New York:
    Thomas Nelson, 1957.

The Oxford Dictionary of English Proverbs.   2nd ed. , ed.
    Paul Harvey.   Oxford: Clarendon Press, 1948.

The Oxford English Dictionary, ed. James A. H. Murray,
    et al. 13 vols. Oxford: Clarendon Press, 1933.

Paradise, N. Burton.   Thomas Lodge: the History of an
    Elizabethan.   New Haven: Yale University Press,
    1931.

Parr, Johnstone, and I. A. Shapiro.   Instructions to Editors
    of the Works of Robert Greene.   Birmingham, Eng-
    land: Shakespeare Institute, 1959.

_____ , and Norman J. Sanders.
    List of Editions, Copies, and Locations of the Works
    of Robert Greene.   Birmingham, England: Shake-
    speare Institute, 1958.

Parrott, Thomas Marc and Robert H. Ball. A Short View
    of Elizabethan Drama. New York: Scribner's,
    1958.

Pollard, A. W. and G. R. Redgrave, comp. A Short-Title
    Catalogue of Books Printed in England, Scotland,
    and Ireland, and of English Books Printed Abroad
    1475-1640. London: Bibliographical Society, 1926.

Rae, Wesley D. Thomas Lodge. New York: Twayne,
    1967.

Ringler, William. "The First Phase of the Elizabethan
    Attack on the Stage, 1558-1579." Huntington
    Library Quarterly, V (1942), 391-418.

Ryan, Pat M., Jr. Thomas Lodge, Gentleman. Hamden,
    Conn.: Shoe String Press, 1958.

Seltzer, Daniel, ed. Robert Greene: Friar Bacon and
    Friar Bungay. Lincoln: University of Nebraska
    Press, 1963.

Short Dictionary of Mythology, ed. P. G. Woodcock. New
    York: Philosophical Library, 1953.

Sisson, Charles J., ed. Thomas Lodge and Other
    Elizabethans. Cambridge: Harvard University
    Press, 1933.

Swaen, A. E. H. "A Looking-Glass for London and England:
    Nutmegs and Ginger." Modern Language Review,
    XXXIII (1938), 404-405.

Tenney, Edward Andrew. Thomas Lodge. Ithaca:
    Cornell University Press, 1935.

Thompson, Elbert N. S. The Controversy Between the
    Puritans and the Stage. New York: Henry Holt,
    1903.

University Microfilms. English Books 1475-1640: Consoli-
    dated Cross Index By STC Numbers, Years 1-19.
    Ann Arbor: University Microfilms, 1956.

Webster's Biographical Dictionary. Springfield, Mass.:
    Merriam, 1943.

Webster's Geographical Dictionary.   Springfield, Mass.:
    Merriam, 1949.

Wimsatt, William K., Jr. and Cleanth Brooks.   Literary
    Criticism: A Short History.   New York: Knopf,
    1964.

Appendix I

Key to Abbreviations

Quartos:
  1. A=Q (1594, Huntington)
  2. B=Q (1598, Huntington)
  3. C=Q (1602, British Museum)
  4. D=Q (1617, Huntington)
  5. Q (n. d. , Chicago)

Modern Editions:
  6. E=Grosart (1881-83)
  7. F=Collins (1905). . . . Q4=G(5); Q5=G(4)
  8. G=Greg (1932):

   G(1)=A
   G(2)=B
   G(3)=C
   G(4)=Q (n. d. , Chicago)=Collins Q5
   G(5)=D=Collins Q4
   G(Dyce)=Dyce (1861) quoted by Greg (1932)

  9. Dyce (1831)

Bibliographical Descriptions:

HT = Head Title   The = Black Letter

RT = Running Title   The = Italic

CW = Catch Word   The = Roman

b. l. = black letter   Mck. = Ronald B. McKerow
                       Printers' and Publishers'
                       Devices in England and
                       Scotland 1485-1640 (London
                       Bibliographical Society, 1949).

Appendix II

A Comparative Chart of Act-Scene Divisions

	Collins (1905) Act-Scene (line)		Greg (1932) Scene (line)	
	1	(1)	1	(1)
I	ii	(159)	ii	(159)
	iii	(290)	iii	(192)
			iv	(290)
	i	(425)	v	(425)
II	ii	(600)	vi	(600)
	iii	(771)	vii	(771)
	i	(951)	viii	(951)
III	ii	(1060)	ix	(1060)
	iii	(1293)	x	(1293)
	i	(1368)	xi	(1368)
	ii	(1460)	xii	(1460)
IV	iii	(1509)	xiii	(1509)
	iv	(1667)	xiv	(1667)
	v	(1736)	xv	(1736)
	i	(1847)	xvi	(1847)
	ii	(2041)	xvii	(2041)
V	iii	(2152)	xviii	(2152)
	iv	(2239)	xix	(2239)
	v	(2312)	xx	(2312)

Total 5 acts and 19 scenes   20 scenes

INDEX

225

227